The Wildflower Way

Fieldnotes for Abundance

🌼

🐢 Turtle Publishing

Copyright © 2025 Claire Roe

All rights reserved. No part of this publication may be reproduced, stored in or introduced into a retrieval system, or transmitted in any form, or by any means (electronic, mechanical, photocopying, recording or otherwise) without the prior written permission of the author. Under no circumstances will any blame or legal responsibility be held against the publisher, or author, for any damages, reparation, or monetary loss due to the information contained within this book including, but not limited to – errors, omissions, or inaccuracies. Either directly or indirectly.

Legal Notice: This book is copyright protected. This book is only for personal use. You cannot amend, distribute, sell, use, quote or paraphrase any part, or the content within this book, without the consent of the author or publisher.

Disclaimer: Please note the information contained within this document is for educational and entertainment purposes only. All effort has been executed to present accurate, up to date, and reliable, complete information. No warranties of any kind are declared or implied. Readers acknowledge that the author is not engaging in the rendering of legal, financial, medical or professional advice. The content within this book has been derived from various sources. Please consult a licensed professional before attempting any techniques outlined in this book.

First published by Turtle Publishing 2025

ISBN: 978-1-7640794-7-1 (paperback)

ISBN: 978-1-7640794-8-8 (ebook)

TurtlePublishing

Dedication

For my family.

Those born from the same blood and those collected along the way.

You have all played a beautifully significant part in my story so far and I am always deeply humbled by our experiences together. You crack me open and nourish me into the truest version of myself every day.

For you, I am grateful.

I love you.

Acknowledgement of Country

This book is being brought to life on Gooreng Gooreng country on the central Queensland coast. I acknowledge the traditional owners of this sacred land, upon which I currently reside. Although this is far from the home where I was born, I feel a sense of home here nestled in the rich culture of this piece of paradise.

I acknowledge the traditional owners long and continuing connection to the land, sea, sky and community. It is with the deepest reverence and gratitude that I live and learn here every day with my beautiful family who are descendants of the Gooreng Gooreng and Wakka Wakka people.

I acknowledge the elders of the past for their strong cultural values and the wisdom they hold. I acknowledge the elders of the present and the future, for their connection, passion and values for they are what keep this ancient culture thriving into the future.

I invite you to take a moment to acknowledge the traditional owners of the land upon which you are reading this book.

I acknowledge my own elders, my ancestors and wisdom keepers, from who I continue to learn and heal. Our stories are much more than our own and it is with respect to all that have come before me that I embark on this journey of deep healing and transcendence of our timelines. My learning of the history and culture here in my new home, has given me so much perspective on my connection to my own culture. It has rekindled a passion within me of deep reverence to my Irish roots, my ancestors and the history that has shaped the stories of my homeland. And graciously, I pay respects to the healing work of the generations before me and the stories that they have contributed to my own journey.

Intention is Everything

Intentions are a powerful force and something that we will lean into throughout this journey together. So I figured what better place to start than to share my intention for the writing of this book with you.

This book has been in the works for over 15 years and I can tell you that the intention has shifted and realigned, time and time again. At the time of finalising this book I feel that my intention is more aligned than ever before and of course with the precious gift of hindsight can see now why it has taken so long to come to fruition.

My intention is to share with my readers, my story. How I have learned to lean into intention and understand vibrational frequency as the powerful tools that they are for co-creating my own reality. I intend to share this lived experience interwoven with some very vulnerable personal stories and the tools that I have gathered along the way to show you that anything is possible.

It is my intention to inspire you to move beyond limitations and to confidently co-create your dreams into reality.

My intention is to show you that healing is possible. To encourage you to be open to the support you need to come into your life to do the deep healing that you require too. I am a firm believer in divine timing and have no doubt that whatever this book unlocks for you, the perfect people will come into your life at the perfect time to assist you on your journey.

This is my experience and it is with the purest of intentions that I share it. I have no intentions to offend anyone and indeed have taken great care to ensure that I am sensitive to the feelings of others in the sharing of my stories. Although we may have been in some of these situations together, our experience of such is entirely our own. We all have a lens through which we see the world. That is what makes our journeys so dynamically unique and interesting. While some of the topics within these pages are sensitive subjects, I share them with the intention of taking you on a journey, a real lived experience. I have considered leaving these elements out but they are an integral part of my story and I hope that in sharing I can inspire beautiful, deep and transformative healing for you too.

I am not your guru and it is not my intention to portray myself as such. You are your own healer and your own manifestation is your co-creation with your team in spirit. I am simply an oracle, here to inspire the ignition within you, of parts that may have been forgotten. To assist you in remembering the essence of who you are and the power of your dreams.

I pray that this book gives you permission to look at your own stuff more compassionately, more lovingly, with more acceptance and grace. So that you may heal too and create the life of your dreams, free from the pain of your past.

I encourage you to take a moment to sit with your intentions for reading this book?

Contents

Come as you are

Manifesting – it's a Vibe	5
An attitude of Gratitude	19
Meeting yourself where you are at	27
The Wheel of Wellness	39

Peace with the Past

Letting Go	49
Awareness, Acknowledgement & Acceptance	59
Finding Freedom	69
Finding MY Freedom	79
Forgiveness	93
Feel the fear and do it anyway!	101
The Opposite of Fear is Faith	109

Today is a Gift. *That's why its called the Present.*

Alchemy in action - Intentional Magic	123
Align with the sign!	129
Space to manifest – minimalism	143
Scheduling - Perimeters for the pivot	155

The future is yours. Write it well.

Write Your Story Strong!	169
Make the Next One Your Best Chapter Yet!	181
Money Manifesting	187
Raising Sensitive Souls	201

Come as you are

Come as you are is one of my favourite take-away's out of all of this healing, to date! I have been on a journey, a deep and profound journey, into my self. And now I want to take you on that journey with me. Except, I am only showing you mine so that you can create the journey for yourself, into yourself.

Into the depths and the knowings of your heart, to hear the echoes of the lineage that you were born from, so that you too can heal and thrive.

The best way to ever show up, in any situation, is as you are. Vulnerably, authentically, real.

I am coming to you now, as an Irish ex-pat living in Australia for 18 years. I've been the heart breaker and the heart broken. I've been the instigator and the finisher. I've been all of the things! And the absolute beauty and joy of it all is, I am only just beginning. In my 40th year this book will be published and in those years I've come to learn that I am a wildflower. Resilient, with the ability to grow, prosper and bring beauty in the most unlikely spaces. And much more beautiful when seen in the collective, nestled colourfully amongst my own kind. My fellow wildflowers, free spirits, deep followers of heart wisdom.

Where-ever this book finds you, I invite you to come as you are! Have no expectation of yourself to have all the answers or to know all of the things. We are only infants in the great universe. Walk this journey with me, with childlike wonder and curiosity.

Lets create space to hear the echoes and tend to the embers so that we may manifest a life beyond our wildest dreams!

Chapter 1

Manifesting – it's a Vibe

That moment when you wake up to realise that you are the radical free spirit that you've always wanted to be. Sure, things look a little different than you expected or initially intended but Wow! When you give yourself a moment to look back, you're way more 'on track' than you give yourself credit for!

It is human nature, you see, or at least societal conditioning, to have us focus on the goals that we've not yet reached or the things we wish we were doing just a bit better. But if we honestly look at those goalposts, really honestly, we see that they're moving targets. Without some really intentional self-accountability and regular self reflection, we will subconsciously always be chasing. Which in turn means we will always be living in lack. That 'nearly there' mentality takes us out of the present moment and in to that elusive "magic" moment in the future, when we have or are enough. I call it elusive because in that lack mindset, with the moving targets, we never quite reach the fulfilment that we chase. What we too often fail to see is that magic moment is now! It's always now! One day at some point in your life before now, you wished yourself here, to this very moment. Perhaps you prayed for the relationship that you are in, you manifested the car that you drive, you called in the job or soul work that you do. Perhaps you envisioned your family, your community. There is something in your life right now, in this moment, that you wished upon the stars for and it's here! That is how magnificently magical you are!

This really came home for me recently. Caravan living with a husband and three small children can certainly have its challenging moments. Our caravan was a bit of a mess! Our little wildlings were running, well, wild! And this mama was really doubting her life choices for a minute. And then I remembered all of the moments in my life when I'd called this in. The years I'd yearned for a husband to grow with and children to love. The long weary days of cleaning a big house that I'd called in the freedom of 'tiny home' living. The painful school drop-offs where I'd asked the Heavens for the courage to home school my children. Every single element of this challenging moment I have actively co-created with the Divine Maker. In that moment, the echoes of my past brought a wave of deep gratitude. And as it washed over me, I could palpably feel my frustrations subside.

I know this can be challenging to see if you are currently in a situation that feels less than favourable but I assure you the more honest and vulnerable you can be in your self reflections, the more powerful this manifesting journey will be for you.

I will admit when I was first introduced to this concept I was resistant too, until I discovered that I had inadvertently been journaling and manifesting in this way for many years before I realised. This book in itself is a manifestation... quite a slow one! I actually started writing this 15 years ago and have put it down and picked it up many times since then. I now see that it needed to be on the journey of epic growth with me over that time period, so that I was more equipped to write it. The me who began this journey all those years ago was a completely different person to the person finally bringing it to life now. Oh how the stories contained in here have changed and the characters have shifted. When I began writing, I was not in a very empowered place. I was in a very tumultuous relationship, not only with my then partner, but certainly with myself too. Having parted ways with my high school sweetheart, I was rebounding in a very unhealthy relationship. Writing was, in a way, my therapy. I documented (and indeed healed through writing) my years to that time. I then began to improvise and to dream a little, romanticising the present and dreaming in the future. Unknown to myself at the time, I was actually writing in the future version of myself. I wrote in that initial book some epic stories of personal responsibility, fearlessness and how meeting an indigenous man assisted me with my fear of snakes. I kid you not it was about 5 years later when my now husband found the handwritten manuscripts and enquired what they were, that the penny dropped. He was the indigenous man from the story and the healing we were doing together was eradicating all kinds of fears! I had literally written him in. This is when my interest in manifesting, the Laws of Attraction and all of this magic really peaked and my more conscious investigation of the hows and whys began. Since then I have manifested some pretty amazing things and become more and more driven with each goal reached. I truly believe that sharing this magic and encouraging its exploration in other people is part of my soul purpose. It certainly makes my soul sing!

Like intuition, manifesting magic is something of a superpower that we all have within us. However, not all of us know, trust, understand, or choose to tap into it. I know it can be scary. As it is often seen as woo-woo. I get it. Although, I have always had an affinity for the weirder things in life. Manifesting saved my life and sharing it with you all brought through dreams that I had long yearned for. To serve in this way is truly life changing. Like attracts like and where our focus goes our energy flows. As a manifesting guide, I always feel like eyes are on me to walk my talk and that in and of itself has been a powerful mindset helper. It can be overwhelming and challenging at times too, but being so passionate about showing up authentically and vulnerably, I use these challenges as learning and teaching tools.

Every morning is a fresh page in our book of life!

The conscious connection with our first thought in the morning is such a powerful tool in creating fresh starts for ourselves, daily. Every morning is an opportunity to write a fresh page and the great thing about you being the author is the creative license; this moment that you're writing right now, doesn't have to look anything like the last. What an empowering realisation! Starting our day with this empowered realisation at the centre of our focus can really amplify the changes we are working on.

I used to wake telling myself how tired I was after another sleep deprived night of new twin mammy life. It was like my husband and I were in competition to determine who was most tired and I needed to have that fully integrated in my body to win! What an absolute nightmare those few months were. Instead of truly enjoying the new mama moments, I was busy creating a story of exhaustion and exasperation. I was so grateful when this was pointed out to me by a dear friend and I had the opportunity to really look at the reality I was creating for myself. This tired mama wasn't achieving any of the things that my heart so desired; I needed to change my story and fast. I started gently, reminding myself each morning of all of the gratitude I felt; a safe home, healthy babies who could cry and need feeding so much during the night, warmth, comfy clothes and a nurturing space, a supportive husband, a good inner circle, hot cuppas, nourishing food. It didn't take long at all until that exhaustion fog started to lift. Disclaimer here, anyone who is active in my life right now knows, sleep still isn't our strong point and some mornings I wake up with that old resentful story. For the most part though I am conscious of finding gratitude first thing and commencing my day with a loving heart. I remember in the beginning this felt so unnatural and quite inauthentic. I still felt tired but I noticed subtle changes in my energy that encouraged me to keep going with this conscious thought practice. It wasn't long before I felt more comfortable in it and my attitude of gratitude began to be rewarded or matched with more experiences to be grateful for.

Be Brave in the pursuit of your dreams!

Something that can often be overlooked when looking in on a manifestation journey from the outside is the bravery, commitment and surrender required to bring these manifestations to life. I use our most recent big manifestations as an example of this. 2 years ago we sold our house and followed our hearts in relocating to my husbands traditional lands. We didn't have a full picture, just an undeniable intuitive nudge that we needed to do this and that everything would unfold in divine timing. We had been feeling that guidance for a time and it was a random happening across a show on TV that sealed the deal for us. My husbands uncle and cousin were speaking on the show and showcasing the absolute breathtaking beauty of this place. That was our final nudge. We called the real estate, prepared our house and began the energetic work of calling this manifestation forward. Now I would be lying if I said there weren't many moments that we needed to stop and check ourselves. Had we completely lost our minds? We were leaving all that was familiar and heading in to some great unknown. We needed to pull out all stops with mindset, self accountability and conscious faith and surrender. "We know we are cared for", "we trust our guidance", "we are safe" are a few of the affirmations I remember leaning into a lot. As we expected, everything unfolded in divine timing and we found ourselves very much at home, in the beautiful coastal town of Agnes Water. Community was one of the biggest things we were calling in and woah! did the universe deliver. So many people who watched this transition unfold have told me how jealous they are of our new life. I need to be honest, I have been pretty triggered by that. My message to anyone who finds themselves feeling jealous is simple. Don't be. Choose to channel that energy into your own dreams. Jealousy is a lower vibrational frequency. Change your state and remember that where your focus goes your energy flows. Ditch the envy and focus on the energies that you want to create in your life, match the frequency of what you are calling in. This is not by any means saying 'fake it till you make it' instead focus on raising your vibe. Remembering that authenticity is key. If you feel the shadows; heal it.

This is something that we worked for, we committed to. We exercised bravery, surrender and faith like never before. We didn't just land here, well we did, but first we had to jump. We had to commit to that surrender and flow. We live daily in awareness of our energetic vibe, of our focus, with gratitude, connection to our intuition, commitment to our healing. It is an ever-evolving journey.

That level of control can be confronting!

Trust me I get this. I avoided for a long time, and as I share my story here, you'll come to see that I was a slow learner. The issue was I was too often focusing on things outside of my control and exhausting myself trying to fix things in that realm.

When I learned to work within the parameters of this, my alchemy game became phenomenally stronger and when I learned to only focus on what was within my control; my manifestations, my co-creations with the universe really took flight. Using the tools that I share with you here in this book, I finally got off the hamster wheel of repeated cycles and began to create new stories for myself.

None of it is classified, it's not some 'secret' recipe. It is life learnings and I love to share what I know, when and where I can. We all absolutely have the power to manifest the life desire. It will almost certainly require some sacrifice along the way but that is where regularly tapping into some very important questions are vital.

- ~ Does this align with the life that I am trying to create?
- ~ What do I value?
- ~ How can I commit to higher frequency energy in this moment?
- ~ What is holding me back right now?

Don't worry about it if you don't know the answer to those questions in this moment. Or as I used to, feel completely overwhelmed even trying to define a value. As we journey through these chapters together, all of this will become more and more clear. Our mission is clarity, it is unlocking the manifesting potential within you and adopting a more empowered approach to manifesting your dreams.

Control is not our only empowerment ally here. Lets bring our awareness now to Choice Theory. Understanding Choice Theory can be confronting, especially if we are feeling less than optimally empowered. In more challenging moments, it can be a tricky pill to swallow to sit with the understanding that we have chosen and manifested this life for ourselves. When we can see this as a super power, the dramatic perspective shift that results from this radical self responsibility is incredible. What are we learning in this moment? Choice Theory can take us from victim to empowerment in an instant. If what we are currently experiencing is not in line with our deepest desires, we have, in this moment, an opportunity to make different choices. You know that old chestnut 'you can't keep doing the same thing and expecting different results'. If you are serious about manifesting your best life, it is important for you to understand the role of radical responsibility. Our life is ultimately the culmination of a series of small choices that we've made. So never underestimate the power of even the slightest realignments.

A simple way to connect with Choice Theory is to become aware of the choices we are making day to day and asking yourself if it is truly aligned with the life that you are wishing to create. Knowing, understanding and aligning with our values is all tied in with this too. When we are clear on our values, living in alignment with them is a much easier feat. We will delve into that in a later chapter. For now, I invite you to consider the role that control and choice theory currently play in your world.

Flowing with frequency

We are energetic beings, here having a human experience. Our vibe, vibrational energy, frequency is such a key player in creating a life that feels incredible and aligned. Lower vibrational energies; fear, anger, shame, lack, hate, gossip keep our vibes down and incredibly reduce our manifesting power.

Higher vibrational frequencies; love, gratitude, grace, surrender, acceptance all raise our vibes and significantly increase our manifesting abilities. There are many things that impact our vibrational frequencies and the more aware we are of them, the more consciously we can choose what we allow and welcome into our energetic field. There's that choice theory again! Our frequency is constantly on; we are resonating with the world around us in all of our interactions, whether consciously or not. Every interaction effects our frequency, in either a positive resonant way or a negative or misaligned way.

Lets have a look at 7 things that affect your vibrational frequency:

The Thoughts

We've all heard it, our mindset is central to how we show up in our lives. If our mindset is lacking or malnourished we will constantly find ourselves in situations that are misaligned to the direction that we wish our lives to go in. We've explored this a little earlier with our first thought... but it's not just on waking. Every thought, every story we allow to air in our mind impacts our vibrational frequency.

The Company we Keep

Is it your vibe attracts your tribe or vice versa? Truly though, we've all experienced this. We have all spent time with people who are not aligned with our vision or our dreams, who are vibrating at a different frequency and we have felt it! There's a reason that all the mindset coaches encourage spending time with people who are living the life that you wish to create. You will not only begin to match their energetic frequency but you will also learn so much!

The Music

Frequency music is becoming much more common now and our awareness around all of that is growing. It's not only the frequency of the actual music but the resonance of the words. If you are committed to cultivating more peace in your life, I suggest leaving the angry lyrics behind! Every style of music has it's place, make sure the music you are listening to aligns with the vibe that you are calling in.

The Things You Look At

Just like the music we consume, what we choose to feast on visually also has an impact on our vibrational frequency. Reading the newspaper will have a significantly different effect on your energy than picking up an empowering self help book. This extends to our social media news feed, the art we choose to display in the spaces that we spend most time and anything else that we look at often. Having plants in our home and small spaces that reflect our alignment are helpful tools for anchoring in change. These are all things that we will look into more deeply through out the chapters of this book.

The Environment

What we see, who we co-habit our environment with and how we feel in that space is important to consider too. Is your environment conducive to empowered and aligned choice making? Or is it vibrating at a different frequency to that which you are creating? Is there enough light, air flow, and pleasant things to create good vibes?

The Word

We so seriously underestimate our use of language and how we use the word. This is one that I am super passionate about, that I could easily go off on too big of a tangent now, I wont because I've dedicated a much larger section to it in a later part of the book! Instead I will just bring your awareness to the power of the word, the ones we speak to ourselves and to others. What we affirm for ourselves every moment of every day.

The Gratitude

Such a huge and integral part of our manifesting experience, I have dedicated the entire next chapter to the power of an attitude of gratitude.

Chapter 2

An attitude of Gratitude

Gratitude is such a game changer. It is one of the simple most fastest ways to raise your vibrational energy, which is a key element to manifesting. When my vibe is low, gratitude is my go to. If I just need a little pick me up simply noticing a few things I am grateful for in that moment works. If I'm feeling super flat or more challenged, I allow myself a full page in my journal and go until I can go no longer, listing all of the beautiful blessings in my life. One of my favourite and regular journaling practices is 10x things I am grateful for and why. This is a powerhouse of frequency shifting and a wonderful tool to have in your manifesting toolbox. The why is a key element to this regular ritual and it is a powerful way for us to check in with ourselves and to see where we are at. For example, my children feature on my gratitude list every day. However the reason they make it varies depending on our collective energy or what we are experiencing in that time. Some days I am grateful because I got to hold them tenderly in a challenge, other times I am grateful that they allowed me space to be and feel my own feels. Or maybe they reminded me of the beauty and innocence of child like being or we had fun belly laughing together. Our why changes, and connecting with it in this way is a beautiful opportunity for reflection.

Gratitude tells the universe that we have the ability to appreciate, that we notice the blessings that surround us and that we are absolutely open to receiving and co-creating more! Now all that I've shared above is good in itself but there is one big element of this that I have not mentioned yet... embodiment. It is no good thinking or being in the mental process of gratitude, speaking about it or journaling it because I told you to and then just ticking it off your to do list. For gratitude to work in our co-creation magic we must truly FEEL it! This is embodiment. It is no good just listing things for the sake of it. Feeling into our gratitude and expressing thanks for what we truly count as blessings, raises our vibrational energy, which makes the process of gratitude more and more powerful. It's like chicken and egg, a beautiful cycle of cause and effect.

Anchors are amazing tools for new habits also, I use boiling the kettle to come back to embodied gratitude every morning. I use brushing my teeth to correct my posture after years of breast feeding! I use bed time with my little loves to reflect and give thanks. The key that I have found with anchors is to introduce them incrementally, integrating one before introducing the next. I used to go hard out and try to do all the things at once but in truth, when I do that, nothing sticks. Integration is an important element of all of this work. And this is one example where I say, do not skip that step!

Now, I want you to honestly think, how often you truly express gratitude for the life that you have co-created? Do you express gratitude daily for the dreams come true or indeed, sometimes too for the prayers unanswered, for that near miss you had when a previous version of yourself was willing something misaligned despite the red flags. Do you express gratitude daily, or are you too busy already focusing on the next thing? Perhaps the upgraded version or a slight adjustment to details overlooked in your initial manifestation of this reality. When we spend so much time focused on the future that we miss the magic of the present moment. And it is here, in the present moment, in every moment, that our manifesting journey begins. In every moment we have an unfathomable amount of manifesting magic available to us and every teeny tiny choice we make either takes us into deeper alignment with that infinite and innate magic or further out of alignment with it.

The power of the present moment is truly phenomenal. After all, it only takes one single moment for our lives to change. I see it as every moment we are the writer inf a 'choose your own ending' kind of movie. We can take a moment to contemplate the direction in which our choice will take us and as we lean into our decision, the plot, cast and story line change accordingly. The more aligned our choices are with our truth, our heart, our soul essence, the more peace and harmony we will experience along our path. And just like the flip side of any coin, the opposite is also true. If we allow ourselves to lead by fear-based thoughts, perceived judgements or the opinions of others, we will travel further from the harmony and indeed abundance that we desire.

I feel like this is a wonderful starting point for your personal reflection and interaction with this process. So let me encourage you to explore these journaling questions.

Where in your life at the moment can you see the results of your earlier manifestations?

What is your current relationship with gratitude? Do you have a regular practice and if it is not already, could you make it a daily commitment?

Write out 10 things that you are grateful for and why?

For the next 10 days, set yourself a challenge to do the above gratitude list everyday.

Set a reminder on your phone or do what you need to remind yourself to connect in with this practice at a specific time that suits you each day. It might work well for you to do it on waking in the morning (it's also a fabulous boost for the energy of your day ahead) or perhaps an evening or bedtime gratitude ritual would suit your schedule more. I'm all about meeting yourself where you are at, have a feel into what works for you and DO IT. You will soon come to learn that you are your own best accountability partner.

Celebrate your wins! YOU ARE WORTHY!

I share a lot in this book about my journey with self-criticism, on the flip side of that is... celebration of self. Let me tell you, there is nothing more worthy of celebration than you! Worthiness is a challenge I see come up often and it is something that I absolutely love assisting people to work through. Celebrating ourselves can be a tricky thing to get our heads around and many of us will have grown up with voices around us telling us 'not to be full of ourselves' or to 'don't gloat'. I say LET THAT GO!!!

You are worthy of celebration. You have survived every single challenging experience that you have had to date, if you're anything like me, some of those you will reflect on and wonder how! But you did... you did it and you are here to tell the story. You have already ticked the survive box, now it's time to thrive! Celebrating our wins and our achievements, raises our vibrational energy and lets the universe know that we are absolutely open to more of the same. The power of the happy dance! Embodiment is something that we will certainly come to again and again through this experience and this is one of my favourite pieces of the embodiment puzzle, the high vibe happy dance. When we move our body in sync with a conscious thought, we are programming all of our cells to that frequency, move your hips, stomp your feet, jiggle your body and wave your arms... create your own little happy dance or just flow with where the feeling takes you. Most importantly, allow yourself to feel it in every cell of your body! We have found the power of the collective happy dance and now regularly encourage family ecstatic dance sessions. It's not only a powerful energy shifter but also a wonderful expression of self-love. To give myself the permission to be in the truest expression of myself in that moment, has been so powerful.

When my beautiful husband was turning 40, our little loves and I were so keen to celebrate him in a big way. He was adamant that a party was not on the cards and that no special milestone birthday gifts were welcome. It took me a minute but I realised that there was something underlying this decision. When we began to dig into it a bit more it was this worthiness piece that came to be healed. He had not fully made peace with his past and so felt unworthy of any big celebrations. He had a little voice inside his head that spoke harshly, self-criticised and feared judgement of others. I honoured his process, obviously, as much as I love an excuse to throw a party! Instead, our little family created a beautiful gift to assist him with his healing. We created a colourful poster that explored '40 reasons we love you'. I know simply reading it would have planted a positive seed and it's there for him, when he needs any of those reminders. It is so important for us to love every version of ourselves. Every experience we have had has shaped the person that we are today.

It's not enough to tell ourselves we *'should'* feel worthy or that we are some how broken or flawed because we don't. It is my hope for you, that through the process of reading this book and connecting with the teachings within, that you transcend your relationship with worthiness, raise your frequency and choose positive self talk, that will amplify your manifestation point of attraction.

Making Magic Together

Our smaller, less life-changing, everyday manifestations can often be done with little or no input from others. However, the life-altering ones, ones that impact the people closest to us, our partner, family etc, require a degree of participation. I shouldn't say 'require' as amazing things can be achieved even if you're the only one on the manifestation train. From personal experience, working with my husband to manifest has made it a lot easier. It helps to be on the same page. Manifesting together means regular check-ins to ensure our intentions are aligned and that our visions compliment each other. To confirm that you are manifesting with and not against each other. We don't want him visualising a sports car while I visualise an SUV! I have recently been listening to an Audio book called Change your Paradigm Change Your Life where Bob Proctor shares that he writes his vision every morning, then records it and sends it to his business partner; together they are manifesting common goals. I truly believe that energies can be incredibly amplified when manifesting with other like minded people. Some people believe the exact opposite, and that is ok too. Remember to feel into what's right for you.

Chapter 3

Meeting yourself where you are at

Being your own accountability partner requires getting to know yourself really well! Understanding ourselves, seeing ourselves fully and knowing where we are at is a very important part of this journey. It's not all high vibes and rainbows but it is a lot compassion and understanding, even in our darkest moments. I feel like my relationship with this and my earlier inability to explain this well have caused me some flack over the years. Being perceived as 'spiritual bypassing' because in the opinion of others I wasn't sitting deeply enough with my shadow side. But the truth is, no one can ever make that judgement for you. Your process is entirely your own and despite the judgements, expectations or perceptions of others, you are always exactly where you are meant to be at exactly the right time, even if it feels misaligned or super uncomfortable. Radical self-responsibility and self-awareness are what keeps us growing and flowing through our experiences here in this earthly plane. Every experience, every moment is an opportunity for learning, for expansion, for stepping into deeper alignment with our favourite version of self.

I recall a time, early in our relationship where my desire to manifest a life radically different to what we were used to was quite a challenge to my now husband. 'It's not all sunshine and rainbows' he'd tell me. My retaliation was a turning point in my manifesting journey and an anchor that I have come to lean on many, many times in the years since then too. 'But why? If we are creating our own reality, why create anything less'. Now this doesn't mean that we have had an easy time of it since then, but it has been a powerful anchor in those moments where radical self-responsibility was what I needed to shift the energetic of my experience. I would call this to mind and remind myself that I am manifesting a life of sunshine and rainbows. That peace, joy, ease are all routes that I can choose for myself. It is a choice to welcome in anything different and that staying stuck in old patterns or misaligned energies take the same amount of energy as the bravery to change them does. Now this is not to say that we don't experience resistance and discomfort as we grow, that is a necessary and vital part of the process. It is there, in the discomfort, just outside of our comfort zone that we experience growth.

Favourite Version of Self

This 'favourite version of self' concept is one that I was introduced to by my beautiful friend, mentor and naturopath Dania Foster. Instead of always striving for perfection or some better version or higher self, which all too often leaves us in lack. Dania encouraged me (and I now encourage you) to take some time to truly reflect on myself, my values, my desires and my dreams – free from the filters of societal, familial or any other conditioning that I have experienced in my life so far. I encourage you to get to know yourselves deeply and to identify the traits and characteristics of your favourite version of self. This is the version of self that feels most deeply in alignment with your essence, your truth. In the next chapter, I'll give you some tips and tasks to assist you with this process when I invite you to explore the Wheel of Wellness. This is a process that I connect in with often, devoting a page in my journal to muse and brainstorm what that looks like at any given time. We are always growing, always changing and that is why returning to these rituals regularly is important.

My intention is to explore as many of my learnings and share my processes around them as I feel fit with the flow and the story. I understand at times that you may feel overwhelmed but please know that is totally ok. Remember that we are always exactly where we are meant to be at exactly the right time This journey has been created in this way so it can be self-paced. It will be as beautiful and unique as you. Perfect exactly as it unfolds. There is such a beautiful gentleness in this approach, allow yourself to feel into that, to sit with it while you journey through this process.

That is the magic of our favourite version of self, she is full of compassion for herself and others. My favourite version of self respects real, raw, vulnerability and holds space for myself when things feel challenging or tough. I haven't always been here. My old struggle for being in alignment with my higher or more perfect self was full of self-judgement and harsh consequences. I was self-sabotaging in ways I never understood. And now that I know better I can do better. This is why I have chosen to share my stories with you in this way, to assist you in truly understanding the power of self-compassion and the truth of self-sabotage.

Expectation – Frequency, Fear and Alignment.

In my old patterns my expectations were so high and far away from where I was in that moment that there was no real chance of me every reaching them, not from that place. At least not with any sense of harmony, peace, joy or fulfilment which I have come to realise are things that I greatly value. While I was achieving the goals on the outside, inside I was in turmoil. My too high expectations kept it that way.

Where did these too-high expectations come from? Let me tell you, the journey to uncovering the answers to this was a gnarly one. In short they came from fear. Fear of judgement, fear of not being enough, fear of failure, fear of success, fear of not meeting the expectations of others. Now, through many years of healing, I see that there are so many holes in all of those 'reasons'. Essentially, they are all based on the stories I was telling myself or a narrative being projected to me through a story that someone else was telling themselves. All based on fear. One of the most beautiful and profound learnings I lean into all the time is that every thought, decision or action is based on only two things; love and fear. We are conditioned as a society to live firmly in the fear realm. This fear keeps us grappling to find happiness, love or acceptance in all things external. The next new phone, the soon-to-be true pay rise, the next 5 kilos lost, validation from a family member or another, this list could go on and on. What they all have in common is that they are outside of ourselves and essentially fear-based. When we lean into love, there is an incredibly satisfying and fulfilling sense of gratitude which renders all of these external things much less important. We are less inclined to chase fulfilment outside of our selves. Or more accurately outside of our optimal frequency. Fear, anger, judgement, gossip and comparison are all lower vibrational frequency energetics. While gratitude, joy, love and peace are much higher vibrations. We've all heard it before 'like attracts like' so depending on where we are energetically vibrating the majority of our time, the more of that frequency we will attract in our lives.

Something quite confronting for many people on learning this, is the understanding that in every moment we have a choice about where on the frequency scale we choose to sit. Now of course there are times and challenges in our lives where it will feel like we are plummeted down into the lower frequencies through no fault of our own but what I have come to learn along the way... sometimes the hard way!... Is not only do we have a choice but the more we exercise that choice and consciously choose to raise our vibration the more habitual it becomes. Even in the hardest moments we can come back to our heart, back to love. When we catch ourselves in a moment where we react out of fear and instead take a moment to come back to our heart, the result of the situation will be incredibly different.

A good exercise to build familiarity with our ability to alchemise our energy and to shift your vibrational frequency is to practice, in hindsight. The more familiar we become with this concept and especially it's feelings, the more inclined we will be to call on this tool in the face of a challenge.

So, here's another powerful task for you to contemplate in your journal.

Think back to a time when you were challenged or 'felt forced' into those lower vibrational frequencies. In hindsight what are you grateful for from that situation. I'm going to give you an example here because I know this can be a tricky one to get your head around, especially if you are just starting on your manifesting journey.

Come as you are

Let me tell you a story. It is not an easy story to hear, and I encourage you to check in with yourself before proceeding. Especially if you are sensitive to domestic violence and drug abuse references.

I was 26. Life to this point hadn't been without it's challenges but little did I know that one of my most life-changing challenges was coming to light. To say my relationship wasn't great is an understatement. But having worked so hard to 'win him over', I felt I was in too deep. And that was just the emotional side, not to mention the huge debt our 'care-free lifestyle' had accumulated. He had an easy way about him. It was the bad boy vibe that had attracted me. He was the kind of guy who lived fully in the moment, not worrying one bit about what tomorrow would bring. And my vulnerable self fell into that flow easily. I still worked and hard, because someone had to! The credit cards were maxed out and the cycle of more out than in continued. We masked any worry or fear as best we could; me with alcohol, him with something stronger. Naivety protected me from the details that I would rather not know. What went on in that men den downstairs was out of my realm and well and truly out of my depths too. But the fear was there, lurking beneath and edging threateningly closer to the surface. Now, with the gift of hindsight, I understand that this fear was setting the frequency within which we existed. We were spiralling deeper into a dark abyss. One fight after another. The red flags were all there, waving glaringly in the breeze of each new day. The hopeless romantic within me addicted to the potential that was slipping away with each flag wave that we both choose to ignore.

I had dreams a plenty and one day I dreamed of being a writer. The writing of my first book was going well. A biography meet fiction documenting my journey so far and allowing my mind to run away with where that wave of potential and the journey of life might take me next. What I wasn't expecting was the plot twist the universe delivered.

On the first night of my 27th year, my life took a dramatic turn and all of those ignored signs caught up with me. I was forced into a series of quick decisions and a fight to live. The weight of his anger and his fist bore down on me, in what felt like hours of unfolding. I'm not actually sure how long I was in that room, how long it took to find the gap I needed to make it to the door. I know I was there for a while, there was a process. I started off mouthy as usual. Not giving into the fear that bubbled underneath. I always said I would never let that man get the better of me. He sure had gotten the worst of me. I was absolutely not innocent in the build up to all of this, but when the flood gates opened that night and the punches started to roll, I was very quickly shown how small I was in the scheme of things. I was in real danger, I was so alone in the life we had created together. I was so isolated in that big home with neighbours who preferred to ignore the screams than get involved in our drama.

I was forced into making some radical choices, quick decisions and some pretty huge vows to myself. In the pacing filled spaces between the screaming, I quietly gathered my keys, wallet and phone. They had been thrown out of reach early in the struggle. I knew that once I made a decision to run, there was no turning *back. I prayed for that window of opportunity to open up and as soon as it did, I took it. And that night, I left. Broken and bruised. What I was learning, fast, was that ignoring the nudges from the universe, God, the creator, whatever it is that you believe in; was a one way ticket to a big awakening! I made a vow, to ignore no more. A glimmer of faith that shone through the cracks of those fractured bones told me that there was a valuable lesson in all of this and that my spirit team were not going to let me forget it. I wholeheartedly agreed, jumping in with two feet as I always did. I closed the book on that old chapter, slammed it shut and granted myself the grace to completely begin again. I left more than that relationship behind, so much more; nothing from that lower vibrational frequency time was welcomed forward in my journey. Somewhere, subconsciously in those early nights my dream work upped it's tempo and new contracts were made. As my physical wounds healed, I took time to reflect on my experience and to deeply realign my values. I got super focused on what I knew I would never accept in my life again. I had created an incredibly toxic environment within that relationship. Substance abuse made fighting easy, on both sides. I had made my bed with that one and I well and truly lay in it. I could not define what I wanted, because at that stage I really didn't know. But I knew, very clearly, what I did not want and figured that was a good place to start. We cannot always see the blessing, especially in the moment so it is important to always meet yourself where you are at. Meeting myself where I was at would become one of my greatest allies in creating a better life for myself.*

> *"Essentially, in this moment, it all comes down to trust in where I am and where I am headed. And gratitude for where I have been."* Claire Roe

For me, meeting yourself where you are at is all about coming back into alignment. I have certainly noticed that when I am living in alignment, I experience a deeper sense of peace, ease, grace and harmony in my life. We are spiritual beings having a human experience, not the other way round which, we are all too often led to believe in this experience. It is my intention in this section to remind you that you hold the magic within you and to guide you as you rekindle, ignite or nurture the spark of the truly magical being that you are. I feel like it's important to find our foundation first. To truly meet yourself where you are at, you first need to get really real about where exactly that is. Grounding into the truth of our current situation and creating a foundation on which to build the rest of this journey together.

Let's start with a simple task... an 'I am...' journaling prompt

Come as you are

Now I know that some of you may not be journalers, but for the sake of this journey together I am going to encourage you to buy yourself a journal and grab a pen. Journaling is a powerful tool of self-connection and self-transcendence. If you are really against that idea, then sure, you can just practice these rituals in your mind, but I feel there is an invisible power to writing them down. I see it as the clearest most concise communication with the universe, we are human and in this human experience, we are easily distracted. Personally, if I try to do these tasks in my mind, I get distracted too quickly! And despite my best intentions, I am planning dinner or window shopping in the infinite shopping mall of my mind. So, on a fresh page in your journal, at the top write 'I am...' and allow yourself to flow. There are no right or wrong answers here, whatever comes up is perfect. You are simply bringing our awareness to the moment and to where you are currently at. I encourage you to do this journaling exercise regularly to notice any shifts in perspective and alignment.

Chapter 4

The Wheel of Wellness

Let's start this section with a reflection question: How familiar are you with meeting yourself where you are at? Meeting ourselves where we are at is super important, not only for the foundational reasons that I mentioned just before but also because often we set intentions or outline goals for ourselves that are such a far stretch from our initial starting point. We unintentionally set ourselves up to fail, self-sabotaging.

One of my favourite ways to do what I now call a life inventory, is to deep dive into the Wheel of Wellness. This is a wonderful tool to allow us a real visual look at where we are at and where we feel we could welcome more harmony into our lives. Allowing ourselves to openly reflect on each area ensures that we are taking a holistic approach. I found myself in the early days of this journey focusing solely on one aspect of life and neglecting the others, and the disharmony within that cycle would essentially lead to more self-criticism, shame and ultimately overwhelm. This wheel will become a powerful tool for your manifesting.

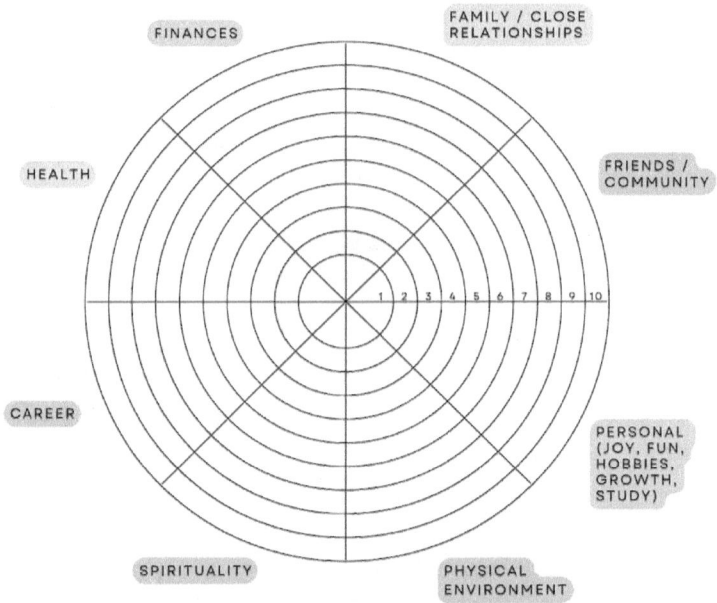

As you explore each element of the wheel please allow yourself to fill it in with an honesty and a vulnerability that will ensure maximum results from this process for yourself. Remember this is about where you are at, not where you want to be. I encourage you to trust yourself and this process. What I suggest below is only a guide, you know yourself better than anyone, so make each section as relatable to your life rhythm as you can. These explorations can be confronting; if it triggers any big emotions within you, please don't despair. In fact, congratulations! Because that trigger has brought to life something big for you, you have inadvertently taken the first step in healing it. Awareness is key but we will talk more about that later. All I want to remind you of now is not to get too caught up in any stories that this trigger brings for you. You are simply acknowledging where you are at and we will work through the rest in due time. You've got this!

Instructions for filling in the wheel are simple: Move through, section by section, read the inspiration pieces, feel into that vibe for yourself and then go to your wheel and colour in the corresponding section. 0 is at the centre of the circle and means that this area is one that currently gets very little focus or attention and requires most work. Ten being areas that are flowing in alignment and require minimal focus or attention. What you will be left with will be a clear visual of the area's that require some assistance to find a more harmonious flow in your life. It's a wheel; if it's chunky, it's movement will be clunky. We are aiming to achieve harmony and a smooth ride!

There are many versions of this wheel available from so many sources. What I share here is one that I have adapted and leaned into for many years on my quest for holistic wellness. You will almost certainly have seen ones that are different or perhaps have one that you feel is more aligned, and that is totally ok. I am sharing this one here for the sake of our journey together and I encourage you to play around and make it your own, once you feel comfortable and confident with its workings and magic!

As I mentioned, what I explore in the points below are intended as inspirational reference only. Please make each section as relevant as you can to your current situation and make it your own!

Health

Health speaks into our holistic health; mental, physical, and emotional. How are your eating habits? Do you exercise regularly? Do you drink enough water? Get enough sun / sleep? How are you mentally & emotionally? Tyler Tolman's 7 principles of health is something that I incorporate here, when I am considering how well my holistic health is!

Career / Biz / Life Purpose

Whether you are working for someone else, running a soul-centred business or fulfilling your life purpose in another way. This element speaks into the soul work that you do on the daily. Do you have clear goals? Are they on track? Are you progressing well or is there stagnancy or fear that needs your attention? Are you reaching the targets that you set for yourself? Have you done much exploring of the concept of life purpose, or is this something that is new to you? I encourage you to focus on the feeling of fulfilment here, how does that resonate with you?

Finances

What is your relationship with money like? Are you scared to answer unknown numbers that call your phone? Are you abundant and flowing in your finances? Are there loans and unnecessary stresses on your wallet? Finances can be another tricky or sticky audit point for so many people, we live in a world that is so dominated by lack mentality, always wanting more, striving for more etc. I dedicate an entire chapter later in the book to money manifesting because this was a massive area of transcendence for me.

Family / Close Relationships

This speaks into all of your closest relationships; romantic partner or spouse? Children? Siblings? Parents etc. How healthy are your relationships? Do you make effort to connect regularly? Is there shame around disconnect or discord? Remember there is no judgement here, no one is coming to review your answers and tell you if they are right or wrong; this is a personal life audit, for you only!

Friends / Community

Your wider relationships. Your friendship, your community, any groups or teams that you are part of. How are those relationships? Do you nurture them as you would like to? Or are you avoidant of deeper connections and tough conversations in those situations? Do you have friends that you can lean on, trust and confide in? Again, don't despair if this score isn't as high as you would like it to be.

Personal (Joy / Fun / Hobbies / Growth / Study)

What sparks passion in you? What brings you joy? Is there a way that you can increase the measure of this joy and fun connection for yourself? Do you have hobbies? Are you consciously learning often? Do you pursue the quest of gaining knowledge in things that you are interested in? Passion is one of Tyler Tolmans 7 principles of health that I mentioned above, I feel compelled to mention it here because I believe it is an important factor that we often overlook because we are so conditioned to 'busy = success'.... well, I say lets rewrite that story! Your personal joy, growth and connection are paramount for living a blissful life and bravely becoming your favourite version of self!

Physical Environment

This speaks into the places you spend most time? Your home, your office, your car. Is your home your haven? Is your bedroom your sanctuary? How does the energy in your workspace feel? We delve into this more in a later chapter too but I mention it here because it is something that is often overlooked in our manifesting or well being journeys. We tend to see it as outside of ourselves and so not important to our inner work, but I have found a direct correlation with our inner and outer worlds. Yes, creatives like a messy desk but their mess is their sanctuary. It is important to know what we value in our external space as it is an extension of our energy.

Spirituality

Do you take time to explore and develop self-connection and connection with higher realms? Do you pray or meditate often? Do you often connect with (watch, listen to, read) inspiring things? How is your relationship with your intuition? If not, you're about to start!!! Spirituality is something that modern society teaches us to 'take some time for', my passion is for making every day magic. Now you can take that as making every day magic or everyday magic! It is one and the same. There is magic in every moment, should we choose to find it.

Now that you have completed the wheel, take a moment to reflect on how it resonates with you?

How does it look? Are there areas that are calling for your attention more than others?

We will come back to this tool later, when we look more deeply at gratitude and intention setting. For now it is simply a good foundation on which to refer back to as needed throughout this manifesting journey. We will put this aside for now and look back before we look forward!

But, quickly, before parking this section and moving on to some more deep healing. I just want to mention, meeting yourself where you are at doesn't always need to be such a big exercise. For the sake of our manifesting journey together, I wanted to encourage the deep dive that is the wheel of wellness. However, day to day, meeting yourself where you are at can be as simple as checking in.... How do you feel? What is your body telling you? What is alive for you right now?

Truly knowing where you are at is the first step to the real self-accountability and self responsibility that are required in a true powerful authentic manifesting journey. There is no 'fake it till you make it here', in fact, faking it is banned!!! We want REAL, RAW, VULNERABLE AUTHENTICITY because that is where the real manifesting power is at! Fake is a fear-based reality, we live in love!

Peace with the Past

"There are two types of tired, one that requires rest and one that requires peace."
Unknown

Chapter 5

Letting Go

To truly find peace in our present and freedom in our future, we must untether ourselves from our past. This section can be super confronting for many people and is one that is commonly avoided because it can unearth so much emotional stuff. But I encourage you, meet yourself where you are at. Go gently and know that the work you do here is absolutely worth it.

So, why did I share such a confronting personal story with you in the opening chapters? Because that was one of the most pivotal points in my healing journey. From there I knew I needed to make some radical changes. I needed to make peace with my past. Now I'm not going to lie, healing that was like opening Pandora's Box. I had years of avoidance to wade through, and stacks and stacks of shame-filled misaligned choices to process. But why is letting go so important? Can't we just draw a line in the sand and move on? Sure lines in the sand are helpful sometimes but the unprocessed stuff just comes with us. I see it like this. We are walking through life with a backpack. Every emotional experience we encounter is added to the backpack. If we don't stop regularly to do a clean out of the backpack then walking up the hill is going to be a struggle. But with regular stops to let go of what is no longer serving, the backpack becomes much lighter and the mountain less challenging. It is so important to LET THAT SHIT GO!

> *"Some of us think holding on makes us strong, but sometimes it is letting go"*
> *Hermann Hesse.*

Notice I say 'let it go' rather than the more commonly coined 'releasing'. This is super intentional because over the years I am becoming more and more aware about how powerful, and often misaligned, our language is. Re-leasing, infers that we are taking lease on those thoughts, feelings or patterns again. This was pointed out to me by a beautiful friend and mentor Melanie Hughes a few years ago and really gave traction to the healing I was doing at that time. I know that my journey with words is only scratching the surface, but I certainly notice that the more I learn and the more intentional I am with applying those learnings the more powerful my manifesting magic is becoming. Because words are spells after all and we cast them every moment of every day, as we will connect with and discover more deeply on this journey together.

Before we delve into this deep healing work in the following chapters, I encourage you first to deeply affirm that "it is safe for me to let go of anyone or anything that is not for my highest good". I encourage you to first set yourself an energetic of safety to do the things that you are called to do. To deeply know and understand that holding on to any hurts, trauma's or harmful situations from the past, absolutely does not serve you. Sometimes, it's almost an unconscious process, but holding on to these things feels somewhat safe, it is familiar; often we have been carrying them around for so many years, the weight offers a kind of familiar comfort. It is not until we give ourselves permission to let go of it that we realise how the weight has been impacting our 'emotional backpack'.

Giving ourselves permission for this healing is the first step but it is certainly not the last, this is not a 'one time fixes all' but an ongoing, continuous journey. What I intend to share in this journey with you are tools and stories that you can come back to time and time again. And come back to it we will. I've been on this conscious healing journey for quite some years now and still these steps are just as important to me now as they were when I first discovered them.

In the beginning this can be quite overwhelming, I remember having to be so consciously gentle with myself and the understanding that what I was healing was 25+ years of 'stuff'; there was no way I was going to heal that overnight. If you are inclined toward past life and reincarnation beliefs, you may also like to call to awareness now that some of this stuff we have carried through lifetimes and each life time we are healing only what we have capacity for on this time round! More than once I have got caught in the ego trap of thinking I needed to do and heal it all this life time; that simply is not so.

> *"Nothing in a single-frame picture of a caterpillar tells you it is going to be a butterfly"* Richard Buckminster Fuller.

Do not let your past define you. You deserve peace from those experiences. Let go of the misaligned experiences, the poor choices, the conversations unsaid. I'm sure there are many ways to suck eggs, and I want to point out again before delving into this more triggering territory, that this is based on personal experience. What I share in these next sections will be difficult for some to grasp or accept, that is ok! I've lost count of how many of my clients over the years started out with a complete and very strong aversion to Journaling. If you know me, you know this is my jam! I LOVE journaling and finding this tool completely transformed my life. I was actually doing it before I even realised what I was doing. That's happened a lot on this spiritual journey of mine actually, where I've done things and then later learned they are actually a thing! I love synchronicities like that. If you hear journaling and think 'that's not for me', I implore you... give it a go! Even just for the sake of this journey together, if it doesn't transform your life you can park it again at the end and move on, uninhibited. Journaling features strongly in the processes I share in this book and so I thought an introduction to Journaling, my journaling journey and what the process means to me would be a valuable place to start, to give you a good idea of why I am so stark raving mad about it!

I was introduced to the conscious process of journaling by a good friend of mine quite a few years ago now. When she first suggested it, I was broke, jobless and uncertain about what direction my wild life was going to take me in next. She spoke about me being the creator of my own reality and I'm not going to lie, I thought she was pretty rude! Did she really think that I had created the past few tumultuous years for my self, of my own free will??? Who would do that to themselves??? I'd broken up with the then love of my life, my childhood sweetheart; multiple times! I was slow to learn my lessons then, that's for sure! I'd had a whirlwind abusive relationship as a rebound. Together in that short fleeting 'romance' I had stupidly accrued a large debt, solely in my name... well played sir! I had lost my job, found a new one that I loved then got made redundant. I was in a new and loving relationship but the abundant flow just wasn't following. Struggle street seemed to always find me and my good ol' reliable alcohol was no longer numbing as it had for so many years before. I knew somewhere deep down that my soul desired so much more for my life. But how to break these cycles, I just did not know. She suggested starting with gratitude and I wanted to punch her in the face! Lucky for her this conversation was over the phone and when we'd hung up I had not much else to do, so I thought I'd give it a go. There was no instant change. No knight in shining armour knocking on our front door with a hefty cheque to quiet the phone calls that I was constantly avoiding. The nightmares of my previous relationship continued to play in my mind and the overwhelming feelings of shame and guilt from many years of misaligned shit just kept rolling in. But for some reason, unknown to myself at the time, I continued with the process. Not too far in, I can't remember exactly when, I began to feel much more positive about my situation. Sure I still had the debt and the constant phone calls to remind me of it and no job yet, but I began to focus more on feeling grateful that I was in a safe and loving relationship. That we had a house and each other. That there was always food in the fridge and we were in good health. Suddenly, this 'positive noticing' began to spiral. Even on the most challenging days I would automatically find things to be grateful for, rather than focusing on what was weighing me down or feeling heavy And the physical results of this inner work began to manifest in ways that almost seemed impossible. I'll share more about the physical manifestations later in the book, for now all that matters is that I was seeing results. I didn't really understand what was happening but I knew it was working. And so I began to look into it a bit more and discovered 'The Secret' watching that and gaining a bit more understanding I was hooked.

My friend's next suggestion was met with much more optimism and she encouraged me to take this manifesting game to the next level. She encouraged me to write a vision. I was now beginning to consciously converse with the universe about what it was that I was calling in. Suddenly I understood the power of that and how much my mindset and my clear communication was working. When the heavy feelings of the past would surface again, I decided that I wanted to actively do something to heal those stories and my attachment to them. And so I discovered, from memory through the same journaling encourager friend, a process of healing through journaling that I have used in my regular rhythms since that day! I began to explore the concept of letting go of the past, of allowing myself to explore and witness the feelings, emotions and stories that came up with painful memories. To work with the magic of the universal support that I was becoming more and more aware of, to let them go. In the beginning I was 'releasing' because the reality of that word had not come to my awareness yet; when you know better you can do better, right? Below I want to share some of my favourite journaling techniques with you to encourage you to also make peace with your past.

Now I feel it is important to reiterate here, this is not a magic wand 'one time fix all' kind of solution, it is certainly a journey. And although the waves of shame, guilt, sadness etc still surface for me from time to time, the more I surrender into this healing journey, the more layers of the healing onion that I process, the less 'derailing' those old emotions are to me. The flashbacks still come, the waves of shame still wash over me but now that I allow them, that I see them and tenderly hold space for that old version of myself, they no longer penetrate or hinder me like they used to. I remember a time when those waves would wash over me and instantly render me stagnant. Feeling unworthy of the healing and the abundance that my soul truly desired. I am so grateful that at some point my desire for peace outweighed the rest. And now I am able to hold and nurture the young girl I once was. And while the flashbacks still come and the waves of shame and guilt wash over me, so too does gratitude. Gratitude that I survived those darker days and the less than favourable situations that I got myself into. Gratitude that I have healed so much of what caused the continuation of those misaligned choices over so many years. Gratitude that I found myself, as cliched as that sounds. Gratitude that I have grown.

One of the most powerful healing journaling tools I lean on over and over again in my quest for making peace with the past is a simple 'I lovingly let go of...' journaling sesh. Now I say simple, because the concept of it is quite that, you write 'I lovingly let go of...' as the title on your page and you let it flow! It can, however, be incredibly challenging and confronting, depending on what it is that you are working through and healing. We all have a past, we can't get to this point in our lives without some sticky situations or challenges that we wish we had handled differently. The difference that a commitment to our personal healing makes is that our self-responsibility, our fearlessness in self-reflection and our desire to transcend those situations means that we are open to seeing and learning from the lessons that those situations have presented for us. We all know someone, maybe ourselves (I'm talking about myself here... an old version of me!!!) who is super slow at learning the lessons, time and time again they attract the same situations or make the same decisions and expect different results. Allowing yourself permission, time and space to let go of the emotional and energetic attachments to those situations creates space for new more aligned experiences to come in. If we are so attached to keeping that back pack full and fighting the zip to stay closed, for fear of our past spilling out, we will never know the freedom of a lighter journey or the joy of new emotional experiences. In order to create a future that is different, we must free ourselves from the chains of our stories of the past. Your mind deserves to know that kind of peace.

I encourage you now, to grab your journal & explore a 'I lovingly let go of...' flow.

You might be surprised where it will take you!

Chapter 6

Awareness, Acknowledgement & Acceptance

When I was first delving into this with clients in one of my earliest manifest courses, I was guided to share the importance of Awareness, Acknowledgement and Acceptance. This is a game changer! In order to make peace with some element of our past, we must first become aware of it's existence. I liken this to an alcoholic becoming sober, the absolute first step is to allow the awareness in that their drinking is an issue that needs to be addressed. When we are unaware of our 'stuff', whatever it may be, we can do nothing to consciously change it. Identify the feeling, emotion or situation, and then name it, if you haven't already. The next step is to acknowledge the role that it has played in your journey so far. Becoming aware of how it presents or plays out and how it impacts our energy, choices and alignments. Then we must accept the truth of our relationship with it to date, remembering that even 'misaligned' energy plays a role. I've put that in inverted comma's because on a soul level we know that in fact nothing is misaligned, everything is delivered to us in divine timing, always. The experiences we have are all part of the greater plan and part of our soul growth.

'We can never obtain peace in the outer world until we make peace within ourselves'
Dalai Lama XIV

Remembering that every experience we have lived and witnessed up to now has brought us to this moment, big or small, they have culminated to shaped the person we are today. Whether we are aware of it or not. Nothing is ever 'wrong' for us. Certainly some things may feel more challenging or painful to navigate but we are always exactly where we are meant to be. What we choose to do with these experiences is the difference between healing and growth or staying stuck in old loops and patterns. There's Choice Theory again! The knowing that every moment is contributing to the story of our life is one of the key understandings to unlock our manifesting potential.

When I first started doing this work, I had 25 or so years of shit to wade through. The first chapter of this healing was a tough slog! There was so much buried beneath years of numbing and avoiding, that it almost felt impossible, but the more I worked through it, the more empowered I felt. With each step it became more graceful. Once I'd sorted the backlog and had committed to doing this work regularly, it became a much more manageable and enjoyable task. My ability to hold space for that younger version of myself with compassion and love has grown from strength to strength and so fear and shame etc do not play such a leading role in these processes. I encourage you to grab the tissues and to let yourself get fully immersed in this process, especially if you are new to this work. You are safe to let go of all of those old emotions and your journal is your safe space to explore them.

If your journal is not your safe space, if that privacy has previously been invaded or you feel that there may be a threat of it being seen, seek an alternative place to do your journaling. Over the years I have had clients who did not feel safe in pouring their hearts out on to the page, for one reason or another. So what I encouraged them to do is to use their phone or laptop. Open a new note or document and journal on to there, you can also turn off auto save so you have that reassurance too, when you're finished simply CTRL +A and DELETE. That way you have still allowed yourself the time and space to be in the process but there is no trace of what you have brought to the surface for yourself. This reminds me of a question I so often get asked at journaling workshops... do I keep / read my old journals. For so many years my answer was always a very clear and decisive NO! I was processing some pretty yucky stuff and I did not ever want to revisit those feels again. But now, over time when my daily reflections have become much more gentle and my gratitude lists more abundant, I am not opposed to keeping and reading back over some of my journals. The block to me doing that now is I live in a tiny space and I love books, bookshelf space is valuable, so keeping old journals is not a priority for me.

Before I send you off into any deep tasks around Peace with your Past, I want to take a moment to reassure you that fear will present. It always does when we are doing something that is unfamiliar or new. We will delve into fear in more detail in Chapter 10. Truly, I don't feel like one element or another of this content is more valuable than another and trying to decipher which order to present all of this powerful information to you, is always something I find challenging. I think every course I have run over the past ten or so years have presented the same challenge. It's like chicken and egg. If you feel too blocked by fear in your beginnings of this exploration, then please do not despair, simply continue reading the next chapters and allow yourself to work through those processes first, coming back to this when you feel more equipped. Everyone is different and I trust that you will find the flow that absolutely suits you best.

Some times when we are giving ourselves permission to make peace with our past, we may find it a little more difficult to make peace with people from our past. Those conversations unsaid and the points of view unspoken can make finding peace more painful.

For these situations, I encourage you to explore the magic that is writing a letter. I always share this with a disclaimer.... You do not need to send the letter. I will never forget the day I got a call from a client telling me he had sent the letter... to his ex. I'm sure, from what he had shared in our last session that the contents of that letter weren't exactly friendly! The letter doesn't need to be sent. You are not trying to convince the other person of anything or to change their part in this at all. You are doing this on your quest for personal peace, what you are writing in this letter is about getting things off your chest, saying those unspoken words, fearlessly, so that you can leave that situation in it's current form in the past, so that you can know peace. These letters are quite potent. I like to see it as my higher self having a conversation with their higher self and on an energetic level the work is done. There is no need for our human to feel the need to be too involved. Once the letter is written and the energetic work is done, we can let ourselves let go of any expectation of an outcome. One thing I love about this letter writing process, is that we can do it for loved ones who have passed to the next life too. If you feel you need a bit more ritual around this process, add fire! Burning your letters once you have completed writing it can be a very powerful energetic process. Please be safe when doing fire rituals, yes another disclaimer based on client experience!!!

Another process I feel is worth mentioning here is more about making peace with the present than the past but is another powerful journaling tool, along the same lines. Brain Dumping is like minimalism for the mind. I absolutely love that stuff. We will get to minimalism in more detail, but for now I'm talking about clearing out the mind closet. Of course what we just went through about letting go of the past is a powerful mind cleanser, but I also want to bring to your attention the power of doing that in the current moment. We all know those moments when someone is talking to us and we know they are but our mind is somewhere completely different. I experience this most in moments when I am feeling very overwhelmed. Where my mind is racing and trying to keep up with the too many tabs that are open in my brain. Rather than getting sucked into those stories or caught up in the overwhelm, I allow myself time and space with my journal to just write it all out. It can be chaotic and all over the place, sometimes my writing isn't even legible but it doesn't matter. It is all about the process of letting it go. Knowing that what is meant for you will make its way back and what is not will be taken by the universe and transcended. LET IT GO... all of the things. The lighter your brain, the lighter your energy. The clearer your mind, the clearer your manifestation channels.

As I mentioned, maybe even more than once, these processes can feel like a lot of heavy lifting to begin with. But like all new things, once you get a bit of practice and find your flow, it becomes a much more enjoyable process. The more you do them, the more peace in the process and profound the results. I am a journaling junkie, I've certainly been guilty of worse addictions in my life! And I do these rituals often. Sometimes more than others and I notice the difference now when I've left them on the shelf for too long. While you can do these processes at any time, as a moon lover, it's worth mentioning the power of doing this kind of work under the energies of a full moon. So while I endeavour to sit with these processes often, as part of my regular rhythms, I use the moon as a personal accountability partner. So I know that I am tending to this process at least once a month, with the beautiful support of the moon at her fullest.

My past is still my past, the difference now is I own it in confidence, from a place of healing. Its echoes no longer haunt me.

I feel like an important note here is that yes, doing the work is important. It's an integral part of our healing journey but what I want to look into now with you, is knowing when the work is done! At some point we have to draw that line and allow ourselves to truly be at peace. I have been guilty of diving too deep into the shadows, spending too much time in the past and truly robbing myself of the beauty and the magic of the present. It is possible to 'go too far' into the rabbit warren of healing and forget to emerge, forget to integrate the learnings and to actually embody the peace in your presence. And so I remind you here, that the line in the sand is important from time to time. When you feel that you have truly done that part; draw a line and hold yourself accountable on only moving forward from there. This is not a one off thing either, you will draw many lines. And the more you do the more effective they will become.

'You have nothing to prove and nothing else to be other than your beautiful colourful self'. This was the card I drew for myself from my Wild Australia deck on the morning that I sat to write this section. I seem to

write as the healing unfolds, each part piecing together in divine timing. At this time I have just come out of an epic healing portal with my husband and daughters and have been leaning in to the magic of Nat Mur homeopathics to assist with letting go of old stuff. All divinely guided and wildly synchronistic as always. I have found peace (again) with my past. With never fitting the bill. I smashed that mould years ago but still, it lures me back in from time to time. This time was a big grief process where I was brought back into closer connection with people from my past; the promise of acceptance (again this time around) being a tantalising bait. I danced around the edge, losing myself for want of fitting. Only to remember that the mould wasn't made for me. Then I remember again that I set myself free. I've mentioned already and I'll mention again, that doing this work doesn't mean that the past miraculously disappears or is different but it means that we are untethered from the shackles of those memories. Every single experience has brought us to this moment. I absolutely would not be the person I am now, without the wonderful and sometimes wild, life that I've led so far. When we can turn the victim moments into gratitude, everything changes.

So to task... This one feels pretty loaded, because it has so many of my favourite

journaling processes. But essentially what I encourage in you at this part of the book is to

begin your journey of making peace with the past.

What is it that you need to let go of in order to feel peace?

Can you make brain dumping and letting go a regular part of your rhythm too?

In chapter 4 we looked at the Wheel of Wellness and became a little more familiar with what it is that we would like to call in. You can use the wheel as a helpful reference point through this chapter of the book too, looking at what it is that we need to let go of in order to find more harmony and flow in each area of our life.

Chapter 7

Finding Freedom

Addiction is one of those topics that people shy away from and are so fearful to face head on. It is such a huge part of our every day reality and I feel that speaking into these topics and changing the way we do these things, is one of my missions in life. I put addiction and death into the same category, as I often experience the same resistance in conversations about either or both. Finding a new way of seeing these two big life topics absolutely lights me up and I encourage you to open your heart and open your mind, while I share my personal journey of overcoming addiction in these pages with you.

So many will scoff; I was never addicted to any hard core drugs and the addictions I battled are so socially accepted that they're not always seen as problematic addiction in the same light as narcotics and heroin.

But addiction is addiction and until we see all of those substances in the same light we will never find freedom. My relationship with the substances that I have healed were toxic, they did not serve me, my health – physical, mental or emotional, or my relationships in any positive way at all. My addictions, cost me many important relationships and much sanity!

We live in an addicted world. We are so subjected to and accepted in our addictions, and that societal viewpoint makes it difficult to see, let alone break. The zombie apocalypse is well and truly upon us, the only thing is that we were led to believe it would be more 'movie looking zombies' than the mobile phone glaring, sleep deprived humans that we are! I have been on a huge journey of introspection, self-reflection and increased awareness around my habits and addictions. We are in a constant state of intake and we spend so little time in integration stage which is incredibly important. I've seen this most notably in my personal relationship with social media; I will speak into this more in the next chapter but for here I want to highlight how much information I was constantly in-taking without making any time to slow down and process or integrate it.

Integration is an incredibly important and often overlooked part of any pivot or change. At this moment; I am in a period of integration and truly I feel like we almost always are. At the time of writing this it has been over a year since my last can of coke, almost 9months since my last sip of alcohol, over 7 months since my last cigarette and more than 24 hours since my last bad sugar filled chocolate. I am still adjusting to my new way of being. Having the right mindset and understanding the BS excuses that we have created for ourselves is so important. What excuses am I hiding behind? What fears am I not seeing fully? And where am I focusing on lack rather than the absolute abundance of benefits I will receive or achieve as a result claiming this freedom over addiction.

Now I know that reading these chapters will be triggering to many. I have been held in the grasp of addiction for a very long time and I am certainly familiar with all of the feelings and stories that place conjures within us. I know because I held so tightly to those 'vices' for years. Being encouraged, supported and verified by other addicts with the usual 'we all have our vices' or 'you have to have one vice' kind of mentality that keeps us all stuck there… In the vice. It's only now that I have done the work to clear them, that I see with a new clarity the force of that actual word! We are literally admitting that we are being held, whether consciously or not, against our will.

The opposite of addiction is not deprivation as sold to us by the big corporations that profit from our self imprisonment, but freedom. Freedom is the reward. There is no deprivation at all. Once we can truly understand that and align with the new story, we can begin to unravel the other threads misconception that keep us netted there. Speaking from my personal experience and the many years I spent quitting quitting, without this awareness, we just stay there, flailing in failure.

It is so empowering to sit with this new story and integrate a new mindset that tells us that we absolutely can do it. We do not have to add another failure to the list! For me, a pivotal part of this understanding was learning and truly realising that there is no such things as 'one'. I am all too familiar with that trap and now would never let myself fall for that old addicts story of 'just one'.

Recently I was reflecting on how mindlessly I used to have that one sip of coke in my earlier quitting days. Now, I would not fall for that; if there was nothing else to drink, I would go thirsty. Number 1, because that once idolised flavour would be so gross to me now. Number 2 because I'm too proud of how far I've come but also, and likely most importantly, because I've come to understand addiction more than I ever had in the past. I've busted those BS myths and the old stories that would have had me lining up for that damned slippery slide of relapse, over and over again! The slight chance of 'reward' that used to lure me back in, or the belief that 'I've done it once I can do it again', I now know, through years of trial and error, would catapult me back to that place of guilt, self loathing and shame!

Oh man, the shame! I don't miss that old feeling one single bit! In my experience, that momentary "high" of guilty pleasure always travels with its trusted friend shame. The self-criticism spiral would gather all sorts of chaotic emotions as it gained speed and momentum on it's spiralling descent.

In a world that is so addicted, it is radically bold and brave to live a life that is free from such. While I still dance with integration and finding harmony between being way too hard on myself and lovingly nurturing this new version of self into being, I encourage you to remember the importance of meeting yourself where you are at. What I am sharing in the next chapter is not to shame anyone or to cause any negative self dialogue but instead to encourage a shift in perspective. I share these personal stories because they have been such an integral part of my healing journey. Everything is connected, right?

> *"If your desire is strong enough you will always find the resources you need to get it done" Bob Proctor.*

Having a compelling "why" is a really strong ally in creating lasting change in your life. My children are my why. I see these commitments to healing as lightening their load. I once heard Gabor Mate say *"if our parents gave us this much to heal and we give our children a bit less, we are doing well".* I see every element of our healing journeys as intertwined. Now, I am aware that I really could go off on a tangent here, so I will try to keep it on point. When my children were first born, I was on a mission to eliminate any potential for trauma for them. Having lived and been on this trauma healing journey for so much of my life; I wanted to gift them the (I now realise) impossible 'gift' of a trauma free life! Thanks to Brene Brown and her fabulous honesty; I realised that my initial quest is quite the impossible task. These little humans are on their own path, they have their own journeys, their own stories and their own healing to do. So now, my focus has shifted. I am super passionate about modelling healing and creating familiarity for them with the healing tools that will serve them in their lives. I do what healing I can in conjunction with what is presenting for them. For example, recently, one of my girls was prescribed a specific homeopathic. I did some research and learned that this particular one was powerful for supporting the healing of lineage stuff and that parents taking it simultaneously, could support the child's healing. So I absolutely did! What a roller coaster that was, the things that came up that I had no idea had been suppressed. It was wild but totally worth it!

Swapping the Alcohol Hangover for The Spiritual Hangover

Yes that really is a thing! I thought it fitting to tag on a little note about it here before I get into my journey with leaving alcohol behind in the next chapter. Spiritual hangovers are real for me and while not quite as intense as the alcohol induced ones, they certainly can pack a punch! Here's a little personal reflection I wrote in the midst of one recently.

Woah, here I am again! Another spiritual hangover. I remember when this first happened to me and I was so confused by what was going on. I'd gone deep into the shadows, sat there for days honouring the 'stuff' that was moving through me and the next day, I woke up feeling so rough! Surely after all that good work, all that clearing, I should be feeling a million dollars!!! nope. Not the case. My body is integrating all of the healing that I've done.

It's not as simple as it being done in the spiritual realms. I am a human being here in my human body, having this wonderfully imperfect human experience. When I do the big work, it takes my body time. My cells are literally processing the new information and sometimes it can feel like the very opposite to healing!

I liken it to a hangover because it reminds me of my days of drinking. I get into the process, aware that I should be cautiously aware of my body and listening to it's gentle signs. But, the euphoria of the experience is too great. Like the invisible threshold I crossed so many times with my 'safe level' of drunk. Three drinks was my threshold but by the third I felt great and all memories of past alcohol anxiety or hang over symptoms were well and truly forgotten, I felt invincible and so I would continue... hard! Waking up the next day feeling much less than alive! The only difference now, with my spiritual hangovers is the absence of shame. I know it is worth it. I have no regrets!

This week, I sat deeply in the most important circle of my life to date. I was all alone, in the physical sense. Sitting here on my bed, with a crystal and a card. But as soon as I dropped in I was no longer alone. I was surrounded, held, supported and loved by all of my women folk. My nanas to my aunties, my sisters, my nieces, my cousins, my daughters; past and present. They all came to hold mirrors for me, to show me shadows, to hear my truth, to witness my vulnerability to heal my heart. And to allow me to heal theirs. To hold space for the women I cherish most in this world. What a wild ride. Hours in circle with them over a couple of days, I cried and cried, I crumbled, I cherished, I rejoiced and I held space; it felt like the most important space I have held yet. A pinnacle of my healing journey.

And just like the depths of healing I reached in those extraordinary days, today's symptoms are feeling fairly mammoth. I have physical painful, viral type presentations. So I will be gentle with myself, I will nurture myself and take time to integrate all that has been gifted to me, all that I was able to give. The expansion of my heart that I could feel, physically present in my body! I will ride the waves as I have this week. With a grateful heart and a happy soul.

I want to add a note here too; about the importance of reflection. A crazy sequence of events (all in divine timing of course) unfolded within a couple of months to completely railroad me. I was deep in grief and had lost myself in more ways than one. I was taking one moment at a time, putting one foot in front of the other. My childhood sweetheart, who had remained a great friend despite our paths parting over a decade before, had died. I was left in a very strange space of forced healing, reconciling the past and facing my own mortality. I stayed in that gracious healing space, held tenderly and very patiently by my beautiful little family. But at some stage I needed to move out of there. I needed to find my feet again and choose progression. My own mental health was not optimal, my usual joys in life overshadowed by the recurring grief that came to visit. My familiar old friend death visiting too often in a short couple of years. It was like, because I was vulnerable all of the other elements of healing could surface to be seen. And see I did. Reflection helps us see things from a different perspective, from a different vantage point. It can be an absolutely amazing tool in realigning our energy and assisting us with even the biggest challenges. Reflection is such an important part of our healing process and indeed of our mindfulness journey in general. I create time to reflect often and I encourage you to do so too. Reflection and Integration are two parts of this journey that are often overlooked or dismissed. But they are so important for progress. We can do as many ceremonies, medicine journeys or other kind of deeply spiritual ritual as we want. But if we are not taking what we learn back with us into the everyday reality, what use is it? We came here for this human experience and it is through the integration of our spiritual knowing into daily life, that we experience the fullness of this human journey. It is weaving the echoes of the past, of our ancestors, the whisperings of our learnings here through the tapestry of life that enables us to create a future that burns bright and prosperous. We must take what we are learning, remembering or being guided to and put it into practice.

> *"Healing is not always easy but it is always worth it."* Claire Roe

Chapter 8

Finding MY Freedom

My personal journey to freedom; overcoming one addiction at a time.

I used to think that I had an addictive personality. Now don't get me wrong, that belief and understanding kept me safely off many slippery slopes as I navigated the few that I had chosen to slide down. I have a vision of it being like a toddler learning to climb up the slide. I knew never to even try any hardcore drugs or narcotics because I would without a doubt become addicted. Contrary to many beliefs (!!!) I have never been addicted to any illegal substances, it was the legal ones that had me hook, line and sinker. With their clever marketing and societal acceptance. Drinking to excess excused by my cultural background or family history! What a trap! It was in learning that there is no such thing as an addictive personality that I personally found freedom.

Reclaiming that power, I have been slowly chipping away at my health harming, spirit dimming addictions, one at a time. Conscious not to rush in or shock myself into anything, as I know those kind of 'all in will power' based approaches only lead to one thing – relapse.

What I explore here are my personal journey's with finding freedom from addiction to alcohol, cigarettes, bad sugar and my phone! All of which are certainly still a work in progress. But work that I am devoted to every day. I've come to see that without addictions, without the distractions, I am much more clear thinking, so much more empowered and more self connected than I ever was before. And as welcomed by my beautiful little family, less reactive.

Alcohol & Cigarettes

I am not trying to convert anyone or saying that all drinkers are bad etc. I was a bad drinker. As my husband explained to a family member recently when speaking into his own freedom journey 'I couldn't drink responsibly' and the toll on my mental health was weighing on more than just my mood. I know the power of generational healing and I have made it my mission to heal these familial patterns for my children. I grew up in Ireland and married an Indigenous man. Both our cultures share common post colonisation trauma and the closely linked infamous relationships with alcohol. My inspirational husband and I made a conscious choice to model more empowered lifestyle choices for our children. I do not want them going through life like I did my 20's and 30's believing that this was just how it was to be. That drinking myself into an anxiety ridden oblivion every week was 'normal', that hangover symptoms were just part of the plan and that the level of disconnect I felt with myself, my body, my spirituality, my sexuality, my self in those years was something to be accepted. In hindsight, my poor body had been communicating very clearly with me for years, and I had been ignoring it. That woman laying on the shower floor, purging the poison from my body, in the throws of anxiety, excusing the woeful ritual as normal as I vowed the famous vow to 'never drink again'. Days of shame, guilt, apology and self-loathing would follow. Only to wake up a couple of days later, forgetting the pain, blinded by the promise of a good night. And the cycle would continue, over and over.

As if with a nod from the universe, as I write this my daughter is sitting next to me stitching. Learning to stitch is a perfect analogy for life and she just affirmed that some times you make mistakes! What the gold in this moment was for me was when she affirmed 'I like to learn from those mistakes'... yes my girl!!!! Mistakes are inevitable, we are all learning life, every day. The key is to always be open to the lessons. For so many years I avoided these particular lessons through the lense of another bottle.

Sugar Addiction

While I've focused a lot on alcohol above, at the time of writing this book, I have taken another HUGE step in my journey with addiction. Yesterday, I had my last bad sugar binge. Now I know as I write this it will bring a few eye rolls; it's been one full day! I remember being greeted with that by people on the numerous times that I quit smoking. I remember the same eye roll when I reached more long term goals too, a week, a month, when exactly was it that I could call my self an ex-smoker? drinker? sugar addict? The truth is, you become an ex addict the moment that you vow to be free. The moment that you make the decision to make better choices for yourself, from that moment onward. I no longer excuse relapse or allow myself that 'one', because ultimately, over the years and years of being a quitter I know there is no such things as one! I lost count of how many times I quit being a quitter! It wasn't until I changed my mindset, my language and got really really honest with myself about the addictions I was healing that I actually saw results.

Getting honest with myself about my reactivity was my turning point. I had been listening to the Allan Carr audio book on bad sugar very very slowly, delaying the final ritual of the last bad sugar intake. I was familiar with the process, it was Allan Carr's smoking book that assisted me with being free from my smoking addiction and the processes are very similar. Then one night, a few months into this slow listening journey, I was putting my little wild ones to bed and I caught myself being so reactive. I allowed myself a moment of honest reflection. The truth was their delayed bedtime was edging me further and further from my nightly 'reward', that cup of tea and chocolate was calling me. Hang on, when did that become a nightly thing? It was as if I was 'rewarding' myself for getting through the day, for parenting, for achieving my goals etc. but what if I didn't achieve them, if I hadn't done as well as I would like to during the day? Well then I would allow myself to partake in a 'pity party' style guilty indulgence, believed to ease the shame and guilt but subconsciously just building on them. That night as I sat with my nightly 'treat' I realised just how empty it felt and how guilty I felt about my addiction driven actions a short time before with my children. I started to become more aware of how my sugar lows or delayed addiction fulfilment was impacting my energy and my interactions and realised that I was hooked! Way more than I had ever allowed myself to see before. That was my moment of action, I returned to the book and listened, intently in a much faster time frame, really connecting with the learnings and the action steps. Not too long later, I did it!

Screen Addiction

This section has been drafted and redrafted as my journey with finding freedom evolved through the writing of this book. Six or so months before it's completion I mused how fruitless my attempts to increase my awareness and decrease it's hold was. Of all of the addictions I've overcome, this sneaky one seems to be one of the most difficult to overcome. Although I had been aware of the lack of awareness I held in my scrolling habits and I had taken measures to reduce notifications and limit screen time; I would often find myself idly scrolling as if on autopilot. We are so conditioned to feel a sense of FOMO if we are not 'keeping up' with all of the updates and trends on social media. What was actually a huge ally on my quest to quit, was realising that my 'connection' online was directly correlated to my 'disconnection' in real life. At the time of finishing this book, I have been 2 weeks sans social media (with the exception of Facebook messenger) and what a bright and valuable learning journey it has been.

Here's a reflection I wrote recently on how this journey has been unfolding for me.

In the closing weeks of writing this book; the universe delivered me the 'without a doubt, this is the right decision for me' kick up the ass that I had been waiting for. My page got hacked. Annoying, but also, a really big spotlight on my values and the way that I desire to show up in the world. Having tried in vain to sort it out over a few days, I spent some time reflecting on what this was really presenting for me. It was giving me an opportunity to truly look at some guidance that had been trickling in. I knew there was a more aligned way to be connecting with my readers, one that honoured my transition into 'author', that allowed more space for longer musings and more juicy shares. One where only the people who want to read will receive, rather than adding to the constant and overwhelming influx of information that we all receive through those platforms. Wow! That was an insight I hadn't been expecting. I was so constantly in taking information that nothing was sticking. I was watching all of these reels on conscious parenting and homeschooling but integrating or acting on very very little of it. I explained to a friend just the other night that I was 'too busy' watching my friends children through a screen to watch my own right in front of me. Yuck! I remember recently discussing with my beautiful little loves that I was aware I was spending too much time on my phone and that was something I was working on; they became my greatest accountability partners. They would very clearly remind my that my phone was taking all of my attention again and despite their powerful reminders, a few minutes later I would mindlessly reach for my phone again. I hated how I was showing up for them (or not!) and the self loathing and self criticism just became louder and louder. This constant internal battle between the life I wanted to be living, what I knew in every cell of my being was right for me (alignment) and this addicted dopamine seeking behaviour that disconnected me from life too too much (misalignment). And so I decided this would be the next addiction I would overcome. I used my business page as an excuse for such a long time but the guidance this time was too strong and it was my business page not my personal one that was hacked, the universe weren't holding back the punches this time. I knew we meant business!! So I deleted the apps and vowed to only check in on my biz accounts during 'work times' on the laptop. Oh yes! That felt so good. But wait, I forgot to check the time for that event before I left. All good I'll just quickly log on through my internet browser, just for that one thing. Then the next thing. Suddenly my internet browser replaced the app. And I was still well and truly hooked. As I sat explaining my struggle to my husband, I absent mindedly picked up my phone and started scrolling; a habit that I'd been so hyper aware of and incredibly annoyed by for some time now! Yet here I was, doing it again. That was it, I knew I needed more drastic action. So I logged out and deleted the tab from my browser. It's been two days now. The first day I think I checked my emails about 50 times; there was no feed to scroll, no reels to mindlessly lose myself in. Wow, how many times a day did I just mindlessly pick up my phone to scroll? How much time had I spent in that digital world instead of this real one. It is crazy and horrifying to witness that in myself. I feel so much better every hour that passes without it. Yes there were some benefits, but truly for me it was anti-social media not social media. It was taking all of my attention and productivity. I swear this book would have been finished months ago if I'd put my phone down then!!

Even just detoxing your news feed can have an incredibly powerful impact on your mindset and well-being.

I remember doing this experiment with my husband early in our relationship. I had been observing our phone usage in relation to our moods and behaviours. We were in this habit of getting home in the evening and sitting together to have a beer or two before cooking dinner. We would both pick up our phones and idle scroll while having tidbits of chat about our day. I noticed that hubby would be significantly less chirpy after his scroll time and so one day decided that we would swap phones and see what each other are receiving on our news feeds. I already was consciously following more high vibrational content and minimising things that dulled my vibe. I had been on this conscious connection journey for a bit and hadn't really noticed what a huge impact it had on me until that day. It was somewhat normal for me now and when I swapped and was scrolling hubby's news feed instead, I could really feel my vibrational frequency diminish. The content on his 'feed' was energy draining instead of energy enhancing; so much so that it was truly palpable. Since then I have been even more conscious of what I allow on my 'feed', it is what I am feeding my vibe, my brain, my spirit. I used to feel guilty deleting people *or disconnecting from groups, but now I know the power of those energies, I am much less apologetic.*

I became super aware of this when our teenage daughter first got her phone and was new to Instagram. The expectations that these platforms create in our subconscious mind whether we intend to or not is so powerful. The not quite measuring up, the not _ enough, or too _ is just constantly being fed to us through content that creates unrealistic expectations. It is much harder to stay in our own lane when we are constantly being fed content from others. Comparison begins to creep in, no matter how aware and mindful we are. We are all more aware now that what we see on our feeds is not exactly the full picture, and that life on the reels is a far cry from life behind the camera. When we fall into comparison we must remember that we are only seeing part of the picture and also that comparison is only hurting ourselves; come back to your heart, back to gratitude. My husband always reminds me that comparison is the thief of joy. We all do it from time to time, our current social constructs are created that way. Although, for me that simply was not enough. Even with a positive and empowering news feed, the negative impact on my emotional well-being and my inner voice was too much. I would find myself in comparison too often.

Now, I'm not saying that social media is the only place that we are exposed to comparison, and so I want to go off on a little tangent of comparison healing that I have been working on recently. To compare ourselves to others, to try and 'keep up with the Jones'! I've learned to alchemise this and the power in that shift is mind-blowing. If you find yourself comparing yourself to someone else, look at what it is about them that is sparking this within you and then find gratitude for the unique version of that within yourself. I can only think of a really cliche kind of example of this right now but I'm adding it because this is the flow and I honour that. When I see someone with a flatter tummy or skinnier body than mine, I return to gratitude for my curves.

Taking us off focus

Being mindful of our usage, time and energy is a vital part of this manifesting journey. And indeed our journey to better self care in general. Spending too much time on devices simply distracts us, takes our focus away and overwhelms our psyche – all of which ultimately goes against the principles of manifesting. Remember where your focus goes your energy flows. If you are feeling jealous of some insta persona or less creative than a Pintrest poster; you are affirming those states into your manifesting field. Although it may seem insignificant or unrelated, a five min scroll can have an incredible effect on our manifesting potential. Likewise is true; five mins of conscious scrolling could inspire, encourage and motivate you in amazing ways too. But if we are overloaded with information we are in a constant state of intake with little or no processing or integration.

It has been a wild journey, with incredibly powerful self-reflection, deep learning and profound healing. Revising the book and reading what I wrote before, I realise that although somewhat in my awareness, that comparison and subliminal messaging was playing a much greater role in my mental health decline than I had been aware of 6 months ago. As I said above, I have long been passionate about ensuring that my news feeds were 'higher vibrational' etc, but the comparison piece is something that I just could not escape. Another, slightly tangent, recent learning around this was the poor processing of information that results from doom scrolling. I had so much great value in my feed but I was simply taking in so much informational input that there was simply no way I could possibly process and integrate the true value of what I was learning. There was simply too much. Synchronistically, two audio books that I've listened to this week affirmed the same. We must be aware of the volume of informational input if we are to truly integrate the wisdom within what we are consuming. (Those books for anyone interested are The Science of Getting Rich by Wallace D Wattles and Change Your Paradigm, Change Your Life by Bob Proctor).

Always listening, always learning, always a student of life!

Integrating Freedom

I used to dread 'challenging' situations when I thought about quitting or being without my 'vices'. I'm not even kidding when I say that now I look forward to those opportunities. It's like an extra confirmation for myself that I am truly free. It feels so good to be free. It is so important to celebrate the wins, to allow yourself to feel good, to be proud of your achievements. I remember within a month of vowing to have had my last alcoholic drink, I was met with a tragic and sudden passing of someone I loved. That would have been a totally valid excuse for a previous version of myself to reach for a bottle. But I held strong. I was too proud of the progress that I'd made and I knew that if I could get through this difficult time sans alcohol, then I was finally, truly free! Those weeks were tough in all manners of ways. But when I woke up the day after that funeral, alcohol free, I knew beyond any doubt that I was no longer addicted. Smoking was next and with the confidence that experience had filled me with, I had my last cigarette, I binged on the Allan Carr book on the long drive home and woke up the next morning smoke free! I see now that I had made that commitment to stop drinking in absolute divine timing, of course. I will be honest, even I was surprised that I honoured that commitment despite the emotional challenges. I know now, that I would never allow alcohol a place at any significant moments in life; especially ones that are particularly emotionally charged. I hold too many ugly memories and too many horror stories in my memory bank around losing control with alcohol at pivotal times of my life. There are many many hard nights that I would do so differently now! All perfect of course. But the 'loose lips' is one ghost that I carry with me every day to remind me to live more deeply in alignment with my truth and my values. I am not proud of those alcohol fuelled moments, but I do hold that young girl tenderly, in love. Because of her and all of these hard lessons, I can live in much deeper alignment with my truth and honour her tough learnings with better choices.

    I allowed myself slightly longer integrating that shift. By that stage I had changed quite a bit of my 'social habit' and knew I needed to be gentle with myself. A few months later it was my birthday and I felt I was ready, I allowed myself to organise a cocktail afternoon at my favourite cocktail bar with friends and thoroughly enjoyed sipping mock tails, smoke free. Celebrating life with so many people I love. Celebrations shift gear without the influence of addiction and rather than spending my time relegated out to the smoking area, missing out on the event that I am actually attending. I am in the thick of it, in JOY and having fun. What I used to see as a challenge, I now see as an opportunity.

I highly recommend Allan Carr's range of 'Easy Way' books, I found listening to them much more effective than reading. If you decide to claim your freedom and need a cheerleader, reach out! I am always happy to encourage and guide you through those early days.

If I can do it, you absolutely can too!

Chapter 9

Forgiveness

This is one element of making peace with the past that it took me a little while to get my head around. For what felt like years and years I'd been doing all the journaling, the letting go, even the forgiveness! But something just wasn't shifting, it was like layers were being peeled back and the energy was shifting but there was still a tether there, to that old experience. Finally, one day, the penny dropped. I had forgiven everyone else, except myself. This was especially powerful for that crappy relationship that changed my life! I had forgiven my ex, his brother, the neighbours who 'didn't interfere' time and time again. And still, I felt that there was always more to be done. I was frustrated and beginning to resign myself to the fact that maybe some situations just don't ever find resolve. And then, in a meditation one day, I learned the key... forgiveness of self.

Like most elements of this journey, forgiveness is a very personal thing. There are dictionary definitions that can help us to understand the sentiment of the word but the true feeling of forgiveness is something that we must feel out for ourselves. And that is where I direct clients as a starting point for this journey. I encourage them, and now you, to take a moment to sit with that word and feel into what it means for you. You may even want to journal it out to let those thoughts flow and a picture of personal forgiveness to form.

The dictionary definitions are:

Forgiveness – the action or process of forgiving or being forgiven.

Forgiving – ready and willing to forgive.

Forgive – stop feeling angry or resentful towards someone for an offence, flaw or mistake.

They are simple words but so profound and powerful. The key for me in those definitions is the feeling, Forgiveness is awarding yourself an opportunity to heal your feelings toward a person or situation. It is a much more personal journey that I ever understood. When I first began my forgiveness journey, I had much to forgive. I worked tirelessly through the list of people and situations that I felt needed this energy. As we progress on this healing journey we become increasingly aware of the importance of not blaming people (including ourselves) for things we didn't know. When we know better, we can do better. Our previous versions of self were operating at their best capacity, even if, on reflection it feels a world away from where we are now. Blame dis-empowers us. It takes away our personal responsibility and indeed our personal power. By staying in a place of blame we are continually giving our power away. Forgiveness for me is a power move; it is saying, very clearly, that I am in the driver seat and that I no longer want the heaviness of that situation in the passenger seat. There is a graciousness in forgiveness and when you truly master it, you are liberated from the pain of those experiences.

I say when you truly master it because, through personal experience, I feel that forgiveness can take some time to master. For me it is often a work in progress and something that I sometimes, have to push hard to achieve. This is one place where I do condone that 'fake it till you make it' kind of mentality, only because trying it on and finding your fit is the only way to master this often elusive attribute. When I first began my forgiveness rituals I was saying that I forgave certain people for certain things, including myself. But no matter how convincing I tried to be, I could see through the lies. Forgiveness was hard, like trying to catch a slippery eel with my bare hands, and not only was I not skilled at it, I was also not practised. I felt into its power and knew it was worth the effort so I practised and practised and practised. I found myself finding things to forgive that were easier to forgive so I could flex that muscle and build it's strength. And I did. Over time, I became so comfortable and familiar with the beauty and grace of forgiveness that I began to extend it to more difficult situation in my life and yesssss.... Finally, I began to see the results. Or I should say, feel the results. It was like the final cog in the machine was finally oiled and operating harmoniously with the other components.

The peace and grace that forgiveness affords is not something I want to be without, so I am devoted to continuing to work that muscle regularly and I find that forgiving the bigger things is less laborious now.

I remember as a young Catholic girl, always saying a simple prayer at night time. 'God bless mammy, God bless daddy, God bless everyone and God bless me'. It was the generic catholic school version of the prayer and I said it for many years without much connection or real consideration for the words. As I got older, I amended it, firstly because I wasn't in a 'normal family situation' so the generic 2.5 family prayer just didn't sit well with me. And as I got older it became a bit of a self distraction ritual at bed time, the more people I was praying for the longer I would be excused for delaying sleep. I would pray for my family (by name!) most of my friends' families, my teachers, my sports coaches, the neighbour's dog! I remember the inner turmoil if I felt more expressive toward one auntie than another or if I accidentally left a cousin out. I didn't realise at the time but the power of that intention carried more weight than I'd known. For me God's blessing was pure love, I hadn't yet learned resentment or how to hold a grudge. It was love in its purest form and there was nothing holding that transfer of energy back. Over time I learned to 'hold people accountable for their actions' and began to leave people off this list. It became so complicated, soon the list became too difficult to work through, this internal battle of forgiveness vs accountability. It was too much and soon the list fell away and stayed away for a very long time. It wasn't until a few years ago, years and years after my childhood night time ritual, when learning a new forgiveness prayer that I came to realise the power of my night time list.

It was like my own little mini forgiveness ritual, without really knowing or understanding what it was that I was doing. This sparked something in me, a curiosity. There was someone I used to pray for nightly in my childhood rounds, but we had become somewhat estranged. How curious I was to see if returning to this nightly prayer and adding that person would shift the energetic between us some how. It was an energetic experiment, something which I did often in my early days of discovering and remembering my magic, so while I was committed to see the results I was not completely consistent. I missed nights here and there but still kept my intention strong. Within a rather short period of time it was like the ice had been broken and we had contact. Not the close contact that I had known in my childhood prayer days, but certainly progress on the distance that had been between us for many years. This simply further ignited my fire and passion for forgiveness. What a gracious and powerful part of the process this is.

What I learned through this re-ignition was how holding on to those grudges and not being in the energy of forgiveness and divine love was stealing precious vibrational energy from myself. Waiting for someone to apologise or right a wrong that they didn't even see as wrong, had no impact on them really, only on myself. It was lowering my vibrational frequency and slowing my manifesting magic. What I now realise is that the people I was 'holding to account' through their exclusion from my forgiveness ritual has long since moved on with their lives, they had long forgotten the small situation that had snowballed into a ball of negativity for me. And so I began to work through this process as a regular devotion again. This is such a simple but powerful ritual to include in your practice.

My favourite forgiveness ritual for some time now has leaned on the powerful Hawaiian prayer called the ho'oppoppono. I had an interesting learning recently when a beautiful mentor shared a story with me about her visit to Hawaii and revealed that there is no word for sorry in their vocabulary. The prayer had got lost in translation as many things do and the popularised, western version of it was not quite accurate. For years I had been saying 'I'm sorry, please forgive me, thank you, I love you' as so many others I know had too. I feel like I would like to apologise to anyone who I worked with or shared this prayer with in its incorrect form. When you know better you can do better. What I have come to learn is 'I forgive you, please forgive me, thank you, I love you' and that feels so much better. There are some beautiful versions of this prayer in song out there in the world too, but the only ones I've heard are the previous version. Anyway, saying, singing or just reading the prayer in itself is enough and powerful once our intention is strong and we are embodying the process. Being the journaling nut that I am, I like to journal it out and to explore each element.

> I forgive you – what are you forgiving them for? Explore those elements, Feel those feels, embody that healing.
>
> Please forgive me – this is a great element for keeping ourselves accountable and taking responsibility for the role we played in it too (hint... if it involves us,

we always play a role!). It's also a timely reminder for you to forgive yourself too.

Thank you – For the elements of the relationship or situation that you genuinely feel gratitude for and of course for all of the learnings and lessons that they offered to you.

I love you – this one is one that I struggled with a lot in the beginning, I was very in my head about it and not so much in my heart at all. Ironic right, because this is all about heart healing. What helped me is the remembering that we are spiritual beings here having a human experience, not vice versa, which seems to be our default thought process. Remembering that we are spiritual beings, brings us to the understanding that we are all connected, we are all one, of course I love that person... on a soul level, I love all of this experience. So, if this one presents a challenge for you too, take a moment to connect with your heart; zoom out to see the bigger picture and remember that we are all interconnected, we are all one, then come back to your heart with this new awareness and explore the concept of love. Much easier right? Don't worry if it's not the first time, our human brain can be very loud with it's 'buts', simply keep practising. The deeper into this journey you feel, the easier the zoom out to see the bigger picture stuff becomes.

While I have consciously created a very valuable relationship with forgiveness, lately I noticed an interesting nuance that I had not been aware of before. I can't quite call it a 'misaligned relationship' because everything is always in divine timing, right? But lets for explanations sake refer to it as 'misused pardon'. I realised that somewhere in an attempt to be gentle with myself, to sit with the disharmonious feelings, to flow through the shadows of healing, my relationship with and understanding of forgiveness has become muddied up with misguided self-compassion and ultimately became a personal pardon for inexcusable behaviour and indeed thoughts. It was like, because I was experiencing a tough time, I relied on pardon in place of personal responsibility. In turn, keeping me vibrating at that lower frequency. And perpetuating a cycle devoid of true alignment. My very essence lost in the darkness of depressive moments that served to keep me further away from any desired state of being, any sense of self that I had worked so hard to become and had devoted so much energy into expanding. So now, with the new awareness, I can ask myself confidently, what was it that was holding me in that darker place and of course the answer was a resoundingly familiar theme, that I have witnessed and experienced many times before.... FEAR!

I encourage you to try a forgiveness ritual for yourself now.

Journal 'What does forgiveness mean for me?' Or practice the ho'oponopono.

Chapter 10

Feel the fear and do it anyway!

My old familiar friend! But this time you look so different, you are not the usual forms I have sat with before. Your face has changed, you've aged. Bringing forth new and unfamiliar cycles, not different to the new experiences of late. Recent events have uncovered new ways of processing, new ways of seeing. Old challenges and concerns interwoven into the new, to create a minefield of unfamiliarity that masked you so well. The confrontation of something so unfathomable happening, the feeling of spiralling out of control when you realise that so much is outside of those realms of control. We are not getting into a discussion on control here, but I think it is well worth noting here the relationship between fear and control. A lot of what we fear is simply failure to surrender to things which are out of our control. We are growing more and more conditioned as a society to believe that control is within our human capability and so much further from the truth and the essence of our soul; faith.

"Fear is the absence of faith" Paul Tillich.

I find it kind of ironic that as someone who grew up in a very catholic childhood, with what I understood as a strong faith, I housed such an enormous reserve of fear. I feared everything – the dark, snakes, letting people down, abandonment, being along, the wide open ocean, being 'wrong', doing 'wrong', being judged. Another ironic aspect was that despite my fears – I seemed to attract those exact situations, much more than I would have liked. Of course later I learned about manifestation and came to know that it was not ironic at all. I was literally manifesting my fears by focusing so much on them that I failed to see the lessons. In the years since my awareness expanded, I've come to realise that my personal experience with my childhood religion was much more fear than faith based. The fear of hell impacting my young mind much more than the promises of heaven. It was some time in my early motherhood years that fear became truly apparent to me. Before then I'd masked it with a perfectly orchestrated disconnect, living with abandon. When I came to understand the Laws of Attractions and realised that manifesting worked both ways, I made a commitment to myself to face my fears and to do what needed to be done to uncover them. Of course many were rooted in childhood trauma, losing my mum to cancer at 4 years old was the fertile soil that any abandonment wounds needed to flourish. Being a mum myself at the time of joining those dots, my fear amplified and the fear of being abandoned was overtaken by the fear of becoming the abandoner. I am so grateful for all that I have learned because now, when those fears arise, I remember to refocus my attention and to pour my energy into the heartfelt joy I feel at watching my children grow, visualising us in later stages of our lives and being very clear with the universe that this is what we are co-creating. As well as remembering to surrender, with faith, to everything always being exactly as it is meant to be.

I've come to learn a lot about stress and fear, and their physical manifestations in our body. Now, I am not a qualified health professional and I make no such claims but the link between stress and disease is something that cannot be coincidental. The pressure we put our internal systems when stress is present is literally palpable. All well being, holistic health, functional medicine, longevity teachings focus on reducing stress in our lives and easing that pressure on our physical body. Stress is fear right? If you think about it. If you think about the last time you were stressed and ask yourself why you felt that way, I can almost guarantee that the answer will have a root in fear. We fear so much around physical health and ageing, ironically without seeing the link that our stress and fear is more rapidly manifesting that which we are trying to avoid. A slight side note here but on the conversation of fear and longevity; I recently came to understand more deeply that my desire for all things longevity is not about trying to look younger or defy death; death is inevitable. My relationship with longevity is about the quality of life while we are living. As a society we (generally en mass) die slowly, accepting old age ailments and bodily decline without question. There are so many inspirational people in our world showing us that this does not have to be the case. We do not have to slowly decline toward death. We can live full, vibrant, happy and healthy lives right up until our moment of death if we so choose to. It is never to late to start… and a powerful and pivotal starting point is getting real with our relationship with fear.

We are so conditioned to live in this state though. We are encouraged whether consciously or unconsciously so, to be in fear from a young age. Its like a built in function in our human society today. But what if I told you it was actually a malfunction. A system error or a software bug picked up after manufacture. Stressed and fearful are not our natural states of being. We are spiritual beings here having a human experience. Our spirit, our soul-self is infinitely faith-full. It knows the unlimited support from the universe, God, source, the creator, that is always available to us in every moment and it thrives in that state of surrender. It is fear that gets in the way of our manifesting potential.

'Safety I've come to realise is a melting pot of vulnerability, a splash of confidence and a good large dose of faith.'

In this human experience it is impossible for us to escape fear and stress completely, our world is literally saturated with it. But once we hold the awareness of only two things being real – love and fear, and understand our capacity to transcend fear to faith, we can become radically more responsible for the role fear plays in our lives.

The first step for me as always, is awareness. We must give ourselves permission to see the fear, truly, for what it is. This can be trickier than it sounds. We don't want to feel uncomfortable, often times we feel too disempowered to believe that we can do anything about it anyway. We hide behind our fear, excusing ourselves or masking it with something else, like procrastination, busyness or lack of time. Fear is a clever master of disguise. Perhaps fear of failure, fear of being seen or even more difficult for us to grasp... fear of success. The fear of success was one that truly surprised me! What do you mean I'm afraid of being successful? That is what I had been working so hard toward all my life! Especially in the few years prior to this light bulb when I had selflessly given so much of myself, late nights, long days and so on, to "building my business". "Yes" my beautiful friend responded, but why are you still 'building' it, when will it be built? What is it that is holding you back? Now! There are a few elements to this. Not just fear but also a disallowing of clear goals and outlines by which to measure my success, looped back around to fear again I guess. When I first sat with this and began to explore such a sordid idea, I realised that my fear of success ran deep. I didn't want to be seen as being 'too big for my boots' or 'having notions of myself',. My Irish audience especially will resonate with those terms. I could literally hear the voices of family members scoffing in my head. It almost felt unfortunate to me that the career that I had been so strongly and in-arguably drawn to required me to be so seen, so vulnerable, so out there! I hid behind a faceless brand for years, seeing and being shown that I was destined for success, but in order to achieve it, I needed to show up! Fully, vulnerably and authentically. Cue the childhood fears amplified; judgement, abandonment, criticism. But now, I had tools, I had journaling, I had awareness. I began to name my fears and lean into the practice of 5x whys. It is such a simple and effective tool for rationalising fear and for shifting our awareness. Simply look at and identify your fear and ask yourself why you are afraid of that. Roll with the first answer that comes and then dig into that, by asking why again. And keep going. I have never made it to 5, usually just a few layers in I have seen the truth of my relationship with that fear. Spoiler alert though…. You get no results from accepting 'just because' kind of answers! Once I understand the fear more I can begin to lean into my other tools to heal the root cause and assist myself in changing the story around it.

So to task… Explore your personal relationship with fear.

Practice the x5 whys!

It all stems from understanding and having faith that we absolutely can do these things. Mindset is key. If your fear feels bigger than you can handle, chip away at it, break it down, find your edge and then gently extend it. Reach out to people who can help you. Remember to be gentle with yourself, to meet yourself where you are at, but also to be actively aware that fear will try to sabotage your attempts to heal it. That laundry that suddenly becomes urgent, or the dishes that absolutely cannot wait to be washed. One of my old clients used to muse that fear sure helped get a lot of house work done at her place!!! It's not fear's fault, it doesn't mean to be such a hindrance. It's just so wildly misunderstood. Fear isn't all bad, sometimes it's super useful, like if we are actually in trouble or a threat is imminent. But building a relationship with fear where you learn to ride together without letting it in the driver seat is key to success.

Brene Brown was where I learned to build a relationship of openness and awareness with the stories I create. Now, I laugh, I can be so creative some days those stories can be pretty elaborate and wild!!! How aware are you of the stories that you create for yourself?

"Fear and faith both demand you to believe in something you cannot see. You choose."
Bob Proctor.

Chapter 11

The Opposite of Fear is Faith

I always find it quite ironic when I reflect on my journey with faith throughout this life time, what a roller coaster it has been. Growing up in a predominantly Catholic country, I followed the guidance of my most influential leaders. I said my prayers every night, went to mass every Sunday, attended Catholic Schools, never really even thinking to question my faith. It was when I went to University to study Theology and Psychology and my faith was questioned, that I began to question everything I had so willingly believed. There were men in powerful positions, teaching but not necessarily embodying the word of God. The fact that I had passed the interview into this university was in itself, a miracle. And on reflection it was in that moment that things began to unravel for me. I remember proudly filling out the pre-interview questionnaire in what I now see more clearly was a common pattern for me. I would lean heavily on my people-pleasing tenancy, writing what they wanted to hear but also, nudging the boundaries just a little. Anyway, during this interview with the Dean and his sidekick, that they scoffed that I 'had been part of some RiverDance thing' dismissing one of my proudest moments, there was another comment about what I had shared for the people I most admire question, I can't remember what because I'm pretty sure my criticism wound was activated, I disengaged from that moment and didn't hear much else that they said. From that day the resentment built, in hindsight, it was a crazy plan to continue to 'kind of' attend that place for the next 4 years. To regurgitate the information that they wanted to hear and to only really participate in one class per week, which was my favourite, Moral theology. That was something I could really align with, our lecturer was one of my favourite people in those years and someone who I remember so fondly. His quick wit and cheeky charm nurtured the free thinkers amongst us as we debated and appreciated the moral theological teachings he shared with us. I left there, after 19 years of Catholic education feeling like the biggest misfitting heathen and so began my quest to find my faith. I knew I still believed in God, but truly believed that God didn't believe in me.

I not only left college that week, I also left Ireland's shores! The day of my final exam, Patrick picked me up and we headed straight to the travel agents to book our flights for Australia. I felt free, free to explore faith on my own terms and to see if God felt the same away from the conditional religion that I'd left behind. I kind of forgot my mission for a bit, this was a whole new world to me and faith was far from my priority when I launched into the big new land of Australia. I had friends to make, jobs to find, a whole new continent to explore. It wasn't until a few years later, when I was having a particularly tough time that I realised how far I'd stepped away from my faith. I was driving to work, after breaking up with Patrick and moving to the other side of the city when this strange feeling washed over me. An internal vibration that felt unnerving and scary, I was having a panic attack. Instantly, my go-to was to pray. And so I did. I prayed for the feeling to pass and for God to hold me while I processed these big emotions, I prayed for the strength to continue on the new path that I had recently chosen for myself, I gave thanks for the blessings that had been bestowed upon me until that day, I prayed for the faith to continue to pray and 'repair' my relationship with God. Within a very short space of time, the feelings of panic and overwhelm subsided and I knew my prayers had been answered. Up to that point I would have said the universe had answered my call, but this day, I knew without a doubt that I was in direct communication with God. I began to reflect on all that I'd learned and leaned into and realised that all of the 'magic' I was attributing to the universal energetic forces, were God. I am what I would consider an eclectic spiritualist; I am open to, study and observe many different faiths and teachings and ultimately I live by an internal moral compass that I believe to be in union with God.

Now, I still use very loose language and I'm only sharing this piece because it is an integral part of my journey. There is no agenda here, I am not trying to convert anyone. What I am passionate about is faith. When we know, believe, understand that there is a greater power at play, whatever name or title you give it, in the co-creation of our life; we work more harmoniously with that, to create a life of grace and ease.

From that day forward, I began this work of piecing my worlds together. How could I feel so connected to this 'other world' stuff that I was constantly told was 'wrong' or 'bad' in my catholic upbringing. These forms of magic were feared to say the least. Years and years of exploration, reflection and communion with these higher powers through prayer and meditation brought me to a beautiful and powerful realisation. It is all God. This was confirmed for me in a life changing healing session with a beautiful soul sister and mentor, Melanie Hughes. During the session I was taken on the most powerful visual journey of my life.

I was in a familiar environment, there was familiar music playing (that's part of her magic, the music sync's perfectly with your experience) and I felt very familiar feelings. Where am I? I questioned. I was at a funeral. But who's? Oh, wow, ok this is my own funeral. I'd be lying if I said that wasn't a super uncomfortable realisation. The tears began to flow and I realised I was grieving; a beautiful melting pot of sadness, pride and awe. Grieving for the previous versions of myself, for the lost little girl who rather destructively fumbled her way through life to this point, attempting to find her self. I fully surrendered to this process, I held space for the version of myself that was dying and suddenly, realised. If I am grieving this old version of self, what happens now. Now I know the whole 'rebirth' process seems pretty cliche, but in the moment of this realisation Melanie requested that I turn over and I was laying face up to the ceiling, eyes still closed, grasping dearly to this process, afraid of losing my space or not knowing what comes next. As I got comfortable in my new position, in my minds eye, I turned my head to the right and there standing next to the massage table was Jesus. Shocked, I asked 'what are you doing here?' He smiled and simply responded 'I am always here'. I cried more and the music changed. I knew, beyond doubt, for the first time in my life that my faith was true. I was not abandoned by God. The beliefs that questioned my unique relationship with and understanding of religion were imprinted upon me by others. Their faith is right for them. And it is ok that it is not right for me. It is ok that I see the world through a different lense, that I am more connected with moral theology than going to mass. That my deepest inner yearnings is to bring the teachings of the bible into the modern world in a way that is based on love and abundance, not fear and lack.

In every moment of this life, we have a choice. Essentially we can choose to surrender or to fear. In my narrative, I say that we can choose love or lack! The stories in our head (which as with my story below may have been created or enhanced by others) may be taking us down a lack lustre spiral. We can hang on for the ride or we can take the reigns and steer that ship in a different; more healing, more heart-centred, more aligned direction.

I had spent so many years believing that my degree in theology and psychology were useless to me. That those years of learning at college were a waste. Until I began to grasp the understanding of this practical application of both theology and psychology, and shifted my paradigm on what makes something worth while. Sure my scope had changed and my vision was radically different to when I began those studies. I no longer aligned with the classroom dream that I had set out to accomplish, the thoughts of sitting at the top of the room and diminishing any free spirit in the way that I had been was enough to ensure that teaching in that traditional sense was no longer my desired path. But that didn't make those years a waste or my learnings useless. I was learning to very practically apply all I knew into living a happy, wholesome and abundant life.

Now I do feel like I need to veer off on a little tangent here. I am not saying all teachers are bad. I had some amazing and incredible teachers in my life. The nurturing ones who demonstrate empathy and understanding in ways that only an amazing teacher can. Some who challenged me to grow in ways that felt uncomfortable and strange. I am blessed to know so many wonderful teachers, some who choose the traditional classroom and others who prefer a more 'world' class type of setting. Teachers are amazing people. It just so happens that for the sake of this chapter and the true and correct portrayal of my spiritual journey I felt compelled to share the irony of how my religious teachers lead me on a journey of losing my religion! Everything is in divine timing of course, without that, I would never have found the faith that I have today. Everything always happens for a reason. Anyway, back to this practical application of my studies...

It was in a conversation with a friend when I was encouraging her to apply an attitude of gratitude rather than to stay in the victimised story on loop for her at that time, when she informed me that this process that I had been using and sharing for quite some time was actually a well known psychological theory. I must have missed class that day!! Quoting William Glasser she encouraged me to read his book "Take charge of your life". I love that memory, every time I write or share it I am reminded of the power of this magic. On that call, I was encouraging my friend to find gratitude; life had dealt her some pretty shitty cards and she was on a victim loop. She knew the things but couldn't consistently change her thinking to change the story. Change your story, change your life. I knew that she had just finished a cup of tea before our call, so I thought what better place to start than there. I encouraged her to be grateful for the cup of tea, for the electricity to boil the kettle, for the cup to drink hot liquid from, for the tea bag. She interrupted me 'but what if I can't afford the tea bag?'. I was perplexed, but you already have afforded it, it was in your cupboard and you already used it. 'But what if I bought it on credit?' she quipped. Be grateful for the credit! No matter what your story or what your excuse, there is always a reason to be grateful. Sometimes we have to dig a little deeper or look a little harder but it will be there. To be alive, healthy, breathing, in a comfy bed, with clothes on your back, etc. there is always a reason.

It is not always easy to find gratitude, I notice it can be particularly challenging when my mental health is not optimal or when I am experiencing grief.

When we allow ourselves time to observe and to be grateful for the small things, right in front of us in that moment; healing begins. In those moments, a new story manifests. In my experience, these lower vibrational feelings or experiences are coming from a place of fear too, they are lacking faith. My husband describes an experience like this, as your soul having left for a moment, and I believe that fear can take your spirit away. It takes your faith away. Those 'yeah, but...' moments are like saying to God, I want to believe you, I want to surrender, I want to trust but... I am afraid of something. Often we get so caught up on the narrow vision of this life experience. We forget to zoom out and see the bigger picture. We forget that this is just one part of our experience, that we came here to live and love and laugh and be beautifully humanly messy. We forget that everything that is at play here is all part of God's divine plan. It is in our humanness that we struggle; when we come back to our heart, come back to our faith in the bigger picture and the larger story, we are at peace. We too often forget that when someone passes and leaves this life that they return home to God. Our missing of them in the human form diminishes our remembering that we are divine beings and can connect with the higher realms through faith, stillness, prayer and meditation. Yet, we busy ourselves with distractions to further compliment and confirm our story that they are gone and we are here.

To surrender to the divine is somewhat of a super power in this fast paced human life where we are told and encouraged at every turn to 'gain control' of our life, our weight, our career, our health etc. All of these ideas of control take us further from faith and ultimately further from ourselves and our truth. Knowing that 'everything is exactly as it is meant to be' we are always supported and looked after by the universe. We will attract to ourselves the exact situations that we need. How we choose to see those learnings is up to us. If we avoid it or choose not to do the work, the healing, the learning, we will continue to attract those same lessons in different ways. To manifest, we must be willing to dive deep into our shadows so that we can clear all that is in our way. We must be willing to deeply surrender. Sometimes we can read manifesting guides and feel like 'this seems easy' only to feel disheartened when we realise the commitment and devotion that it takes. Don't be fooled. Surrender is a super power.

Having faith and trust in God does not mean that bad things won't happen. I remember at a younger age feeling like God had abandoned me because of the tough time or trial I was experiencing. I didn't understand divine orchestration or how all of these experiences shape us and our journey. I used to pray for bad things not to happen, rather than the strength and grace to weather the storms. I remember as a child saying the serenity prayer; with no real understanding of what serenity even meant. It is now a prayer that I say often, "Lord, Grant me the serenity to accept the things I cannot change, the courage to change the things I can and the wisdom to know the difference". Like I said, I am not sharing this as any stealthy attempt to convert anyone's beliefs. I have long said that I believe that belief in, understanding of and connection to a higher power is absolutely necessary for our manifesting journey. Lately I've come to define that a little differently, I understand the power of faith as an essential part of the surrender required to co-create with the universe. For me prayer, meditation and connection with source, in my case, God, is an important part of my intuitive process. If I am not taking the time to reflect, offer gratitude, be in stillness to receive guidance. I cannot take the inspired action required to fast track my manifesting potential. I'm not saying it can't happen without faith and regular connection with a higher power, but what I am sharing in this book is my personal experience. In my experience, this is all about living in alignment. To be too busy or distracted to pray, means that I am too busy or distracted to receive the grace of God.

Leaning on my faith, my angels and my guides in times of struggle has redirected my thoughts and realigned my energy and my focus incredibly time and time again. One of the greatest learnings I've had around the power and importance of faith are when we are experiencing loss. Death is something that I am incredibly familiar with since a young age. It is something that has been a consistent part of my journey. I thought that was normal. I thought everyone had this intimate relationship with death until I began to meet people who had very limited experiences of it. I became a somewhat fascinated with witnessing the process, both in myself and in those around me when this old familiar time would come again and I would say farewell to another loved one. Fascinated might be a word that triggers some in the context of death, but humans are truly marvellous creatures and if you've ever truly sat back and witnessed us in the midst of these huge life transitions, it is incredible the healing, the grace and the love that can shine through.

This is why I am devoting my time now to studying end of life and death to bring a more personal connected and ceremonial approach. Growing up in Ireland this was something that I had really taken for granted. It was normal for me. To care for our dead, to sit with them and to honour them in their own home. For the community to rally around and support the grieving family. Group grieving and faith based traditions are worth their weight in gold I can tell you that. Things are done differently here in Australia, their processes are different and there is a sense of disconnect or administrative logistics that negates an important part of the human grieving process, in my opinion. Now I know that this will not be everyone's experience. Having grown up in a country that is so intimately familiar with death and the rich processes that surround that, I am a willing student of life in all things faith based end of life. It doesn't matter your faith, what I have observed is the most incredible role that faith can play in the grieving process. Simply believing that there is life after this world can bring a sense of peace and comfort to families left behind. These ideas around faith in the unknown are interchangeable. If you believe that there is life after death, that we are an eternal soul, so too, you must believe that we are all one, connected, infinite beings with infinite potential. And so it is. That the infinite potential of the universe is there for us to tap in to in every moment.

As with all things in life when we have support and encouragement with the spiritual and logistical elements of whatever situation we are facing, it feels much more manageable. Which is a beautiful segue into the next section.

Today is a Gift.

That's why it's called the Present.

Chapter 12

Alchemy in action - Intentional Magic

I almost decided to omit this entire section of the book in the final stages of writing. I felt that the mundane or logistical side of this work was lost in the magic of the previous chapters. But then, I was guided to remember that the support in the logistics can really bring the magic to the mundane. It is in the mundane that we live, it is when we can find the glimmers of gold there that we truly begin to thrive. This marrying of logistics and spirituality is something that I really enjoy. It is in these spaces that the echoes of our past can really ignite the embers of our future. When we nurture the glimmers, tend to their fire, our inner fire, we thrive! I often wished I had this kind of knowledge available to me when I started out. What I share in these next pages is what I like to call 'practical magic'. This is where my passion has lain for many years. It is in the moments of magic throughout the day that our soul has an opportunity to shine, the more mindful moments, the more grounded gratitude, the more flow and ease. Not that all magic isn't intentional, what I want to explore here with you, is the power of our everyday when done with intention. The power of intention shifts the potency of every thought and every action. Alchemy in action.

When we begin to bring intention into every thought and every action, we unlock a level of connection with our divine selves, that will never lead us wrong. It is through the distraction and busyness of unintentional living that we lose ourselves. Our intuition takes a back seat and we are subconsciously living by someone else's script. What I am sharing here in this chapter are some of the most simple and favourite ways that I infuse intention in to my regular daily practices. First thing in the morning feels like the right place to start. For me, I am quickly in Mama mode and in the kitchen rapidly. I boil the kettle; an anchor for gratitude for my daily rhythm. If I haven't already, I focus on gratitude. As I prepare brekkie I infuse the food that I am making with love and gratitude, thanking the food for it's nourishment and the processes that brought it here to my kitchen and my families plates. Next I move my body, stretching, hooping, skipping, walking or dancing. I check in to see what my body desires and requires, honouring it's amazingness and expressing gratitude for it as I consciously connect and nourish each part with movement and love. You can literally infuse every element of your day with yummy and nurturing intention. Your everyday shower ritual can become a powerful cleansing and self protection ceremony. I love to envision the water as white light washing over me, a spiritual cleansing as such. Water is a powerful conductor of spiritual energy too so setting the intention for the water to wash away my worries and distractions often leads to some big insights and inspirations coming through in my shower time too. If this is the case for you too, you may find it helpful to jot down some notes on hopping out so that you don't fall mindlessly into the distractions of the day and forget to take the inspired actions, to act on those insights. You also don't need to shower to do a beautiful and powerful white light ritual. You can simply take a moment to visualise yourself surrounded by a bubble of white light. This can be a super quick and effective way to protect your energy as you begin day. I also love to include a white light visualisation at bed time, washing away the energies of the day before a peaceful nights sleep.

Like I said, intention can be infused into any moment of your day. Intentional cooking – learning and understanding the nutritional and metaphysical properties of the food that you are preparing and adding them to your dish or pot with gratitude for their magic. Intentional dressing – knowing and appreciating the power and magic of colours and mindfully selecting what you require or desire that day is another beautiful ritual. Intentional gardening – nurturing and nourishing your plants and soil, tapping in to the interconnectedness of everything. I loved learning of the link between soil microbome and our gut microbiome. Knowing that our gut mircobiome is directly linked to our mental health, literally means that tending to our soil can be beneficial for mental health... you can't get more interconnected than that.

Gardening barefoot (obviously exercising caution in countries like this where our slithery friends are many) can create an incredible channel of communication between our mind, body and soil! Now I'm no microbiologist, nor am I an expert gardener (ask my block fam!!!) but I encourage you to expand your mind and to research these amazing connections for yourself. As I wrote this, fear reared its familiar head and told me to fact check this with some more well versed friends. Doubting my rememberings because I am not an expert in this field. But I decided not to, I decided to trust myself and to leave that little ember of inspiration there for anyone who feels called to tend that fire for themselves. It is something that I hope to learn more about in another season of my life. Right now, is not that time! This is an interesting part of the process actually, as I get closer and closer to finishing this book, the more and more fear and doubt creeps in, in so many ways! It's wild what stories we can create for ourselves if we are not aware and on to it.

One more intention I want to add here is intentional listening – this is a pretty cool and surprisingly challenging practice that I am more mindfully adding to my regular rhythms. At a meditation circle a few months ago we were encouraged to mindfully and intentionally listen. We were not allowed to nod or affirm, we were not allowed to speak or agree, we had to practice fully listening. I was so surprised at how challenging it was. Not necessarily listening, but listening with that depth of intention. I hadn't noticed before that, how uncomfortable fully listening can be, how real our need to validate or affirm can be. I didn't realise that I rely on those 'return cues' to let the person know that I hear them, that I am listening. But the cues subtly distract us and we break the power of the communication with our nods and 'uh-hu's'. When left in silences, those spaces between sentences are loaded with wisdom, awareness and 'ah-ha' moments. Since then I have been more actively trying to incorporate intentional listening into my day. Allowing silent moments in my children's stories for them to figure out their own thoughts, for them to connect more deeply with themselves and their truth, for them to find their own solutions. It is a powerful (albeit still challenging) practice.

This list could literally go on infinitely, I know there will be so many glimmers of gold that I have missed in these lines, but you get the picture. The more connected and intentional you are with your everyday process. The more magic your welcome in and create every day!

Chapter 13

Align with the sign!

When we get more intentional with our everyday moments, we naturally slow down and become more aware of ourselves and the world around us. Opening ourselves up to seeing the signs that are abundantly delivered to us, in every moment, should we choose to see them. These signs can be seen as beautiful bread crumbs on our journey of life. If we follow the dots and align with the signs, we will experience grace and a manifesting magic that is beyond our human understanding.

The beautiful synchronicities on this writing journey, never cease to amaze me. I thought I was coming here today to write about money manifesting. But instead I find myself here, exploring this chapter which I not even an hour ago read about in my morning read. 'Money and the Law of Attraction' from Esther and Jerry Hicks reminds us that our alignment to source is pivotal to our manifesting journey. I see it as when I am in fear, when I am worrying or stressing, I am out of alignment with surrender, trust and faith. I am telling the universe 'yeah! I want to work with you, but I don't fully trust you'. Never before has my faith in God been so pertinent as it has of late. I am currently in a low tide; there have been a few divine challenges and because I haven't been looking after myself and my spirit as fiercely as I am used to, I have been less optimistic and less willing to surrender. Every time; I eventually come back to my most trusted mantra's, sometimes that return take a hot minute, other times it takes a bit more convincing in my nervous system. This has been one such time. I am really leaning in on my tools and opening myself up to the signs from the universe. There is so much fear. I am in the final chapters of writing and the finish line is now within sight really for the first time ever. I feel vulnerable. I feel like I have so much on the line, this dream has been such a long time in the making and this final lap is making me absolutely walk my talk in calling my highest vision in!

In this section, we are going to look at aligning with the signs! Listening to the universe, the world around us and of course our body to shift and pivot as much as we need. I'm having a little giggle now, as I type this, noticing how many times already I am correcting my posture today. I've noticed recently that when I need to show up, when I am getting ready to show up in a new way or to put myself out there somehow, my posture slumps. Literally my body speaking to me about standing tall and feeling aligned with being seen. So I intentionally, with affirmation, correct my posture.

Today is a Gift. That's why it's called the Present.

I allow myself to remember that I am safe in my truest expression and that I am worthy of all that I am calling in. While I continue to embody and integrate these new pieces of information, my posture continues to serve as a reminder, I will move and stretch intentionally to support my body with integrating the message and understanding beyond a doubt that this is true for me. Embodiment is an important practice, I've said it before and I'll say it again. Without the embodiment, they are just thoughts, floating around in our beautiful and marvellous human mind.

I encourage you to pay attention to your body; what is it communicating with you? Do you allow time and space to explore what it is telling through discomfort and dis-ease? Metaphysics is something that has been fascinating me for quite some time and it is something that I continue to lean into and learn from all the time. There are literally entire books dedicated to it and to try and cover it here, in a mere section of this chapter would be an injustice. Instead, I want to share what is true for me, what is alive for me in this moment, in the hope to inspire you and encourage your own explorations. I highly recommend Inna Segal's book 'The Secret Language of our Body' for anyone who is keen in diving deeper. It is my go-to. As soon as I bump my little toe on my right foot or cut my left thumb! I am there, reading her wisdom and ready for the learnings and the healing that are being presented to me in that moment. Of course it covers the bigger issues too, and supports much deeper journeys of healing than a cut finger or bumped toe. I am here for it all!

Our body is incredibly intelligent, not only how it communicates with us, but what it stores in it's organs and cells too. We have so much wisdom and healing potential within us. While I am very much a student of the more physical side of healing, I have been connecting more deeply with my body's intelligence to aid and amplify my healing and detoxification.

A quick little share, recently hubby completed his first liver cleanse. We were having a challenging time then, my emotional well-being wasn't optimal and our children were responding to that in a big way, as they do! The collective energy was upgrading and ungrounded. And there was my incredibly intuitive husband, captaining this ship like a boss as we sailed our stormy seas, a new sense of calm that he attributes to his cleansed liver. It has inspired me greatly and although I am not feeling quite ready for that level of commitment. I am learning and leaning more and more into the wisdom of my liver. It is a powerhouse in our body, not just in the physical sense. But also, metaphysically. It is a place where we store emotions; often grief, rage and anger. I am looking at other ways to support this healing too; Myofacial Movement techniques and Somatic Yoga. Maybe there will be more on that if there's a in the second book!! (always a student, but there is a perfect example of correcting my thoughts and my words in real time!)

What do I feel is important to share here? One of the simple and profound shifts for me was understanding that our left hand side of our body relates to our feminine and our female lines. And our right hand side relates to our masculine and our male lines. Our major systems within our body have their own representations and areas of expertise. A lot of our metaphysical healing is quite self-explanatory. Constipation can tell us that we are holding on to too much crap or things that do not serve us, painful shoulders tell us that we are carrying too much responsibility. Often times, simply asking our body to show us what is not in alignment and sitting quietly to hear the response is all that we need to take the inspired action to heal that element of ourselves.

One really good way to check in with your body is simple meditation like a body scan, creating time and space to consciously check in with ourselves and see how we are travelling, what our body is trying to communicate with us that we might be missing or overlooking through distraction or self sabotage. As I mentioned there are amazing resources already available to dig into what presents during this type of body check in, allow them to assist you, but ultimately, you are your best guide; ask your body, it will only be too happy to respond and be heard. Another way that I love to check in with my body is through regular yoga practice. If I can't reach my toes in my morning stretch, I know that I am holding on to tension in my body and there are potentially thoughts or beliefs that I need to let go of in order to be in optimal health, flexibility and flow.

It can be so detrimental to our healing progress to ignore the signs that our body is communicating with us. I remember going through a period of my life; shortly after my twins were born where I was so focused on them and their needs and everything going on around me that I was completely neglecting myself and choosing to turn a blind eye to the niggling signs in my body. I was hospitalised for the most random aliments more times in that short period of my life than I had been in my entire 32 years prior. If we choose to ignore the signs, there is a good chance that the universe will begin to nudge harder and harder! It's not something that goes away.

Everything is connected. When our bodies are flowing optimally, our outer world will reflect that too. And vice versa. I truly believe that a healthy mindset is the corner stone of well-being. With a good mindset we can transcend even the most challenging situations. Surrender, trust and faith of course are all linked with our healthy mindset. Journaling (and writing) are pivotal in that commitment for me. The power of bringing awareness to my thoughts and actively working to shift beliefs that don't serve me, is beyond explanation in words, it needs to be experienced! And I truly hope this book will inspire and assist you to experience that for yourself.

When we feel strong in our body, we feel strong in our mind, we feel strong in our lives and our ability to hold boundaries. If we are in pain or experiencing discomfort regularly, we naturally feel less confident and less capable. If our body is telling us 'we can't' (a word I erase from my vocabulary as much as earthly possible!!!) it is our invitation to explore something that is going on deeper, an emotion or belief that we are holding on to. We absolutely are our own healers and our bodies are wonderful and miraculous vessels. As I write this I recall another wonderful body book I bought years ago, it is called "The Body is the Barometer of the Soul" by Annette Noontil, and one of the most

Today is a Gift. That's why it's called the Present.

fascinating parts of this book for me was how it also had a section for car ailments; our body is our vehicle and our car is an extension of that. A flat battery on your car is likely telling you more than you think!

Signs from Nature

The signs are everywhere if you choose to see them. Signs from nature surround us every day; feathers, leaves, a gust of wind, animals, creatures, nature treasures; all gifts from the universe. A song on the radio, a 'random' conversation. You can take the signs as lightly or as deeply as you like, again there are an abundance of resources, so I encourage you to explore as you feel guided. I see feathers as a sign from my loved ones in heaven, white feathers are particularly welcome as reassurance from my mam. Although we would need another book if we were to try speak into all the signs here, I have created sections below where I share a few. Like all things I encourage you to investigate as they present to you, to simply be open to learning; search and seek information. The right sources always show up at exactly the right time! Like with all things in life, the right teachers will present exactly as we need them. When I am at a crossroads, feeling despondent with life or needing guidance, I simply asking for the steps to be shown to me. Asking for my guides to communicate with me, praying for insight. The absolute key here is remembering to remain open to what comes to you. Many times we are so busy looking that we fail to see. Remain open, objective, aware. Remember what we receive might not always be what we want, but it is always what is right for us in that moment. As Garth Brooks famously sang 'some of God's greatest gifts are unanswered prayers', another layer of that ever present requirement for trust and surrender.

Animals

Each animal we encounter has wonderful messages and teachings for us; many we can feel into by simply observing them in their natural beingness. A hawk represents freedom and power, an echidna speaks to us about being too guarded and having our spikes in action unnecessarily, a kookaburra reminds us to laugh more and to find more joy in our day.

I always find it funny to say that snake energy is my favourite considering that I had an absolute phobia of snakes in physical form until recent years. I remember when we first moved to Australia I made Patrick drive me out of a car park and drop me off before returning to park the car by himself because I saw a snake on the fence and refused to get out of the car! I now live in the bush and encounter these beautiful and powerful creatures often. I have so many snake stories and will try to keep them in context, but one of my favourites, and it's too good not to share, it's the story of the first time I went camping in the bush with my husband and a hundred or so of his family. It was a big family reunion and my first time meeting many of them. I prayed and prayed on the 6+ hour drive there for the ancestors to please protect me from any snake related heart attacks, I affirmed that my intentions were good and that I was going there respectfully and with love. Success! On the drive home, when we returned to the highway, there was the first and only snake I encountered on that trip, just chillin along the side of the road. I took that as a massive nod from the universe. Since then, I've immersed myself into learning more about snakes; education is power, knowledge is the antidote to fear. Now I have a healthy respect for them. And can appreciate their beauty and the power of their spirit message minus the heart attack inducing fear washing over me. Snakes are all about transformation, shedding their skin seasonally, reminding us that we too need to shed to grow and to shine. Snakes for me too, show up when I need to be mindful or aware of false friends, when the wolf in sheep clothing is close by. That intensity of message from them usually comes when I've ignored the warning signs, mistaken the red flags for party buntings! When the snake appears in my field, I know, proceed with caution. At a time last year when I was being too naive or forgiving around false friends, there was literally a snake in the grass! I screamed and jumped a mile high when it raised it's head to alert me of its presence. You can't get a more literal sign than that right!!! If something is trying so hard to get your attention; there is a message in that for you, don't ignore it!

What other animals do I love to connect with? Where to start! I feel like I connect with, appreciate and observe our animal friends every day. Magpies remind me not to get distracted by shiny things. Rainbow lorikeets remind me to live a colourful life and not to be afraid of being heard. Kangaroos remind me of the divine and infinite abundance that surrounds me in every moment. And ducks, those cute little waddly butts, remind me that I can remind graceful on the surface no matter how fast my feet are paddling beneath. I know there will be many more that I wish I'd added later, this is one that presents and extends for me daily. We have little birds land on our windows almost daily, all with different messages. I live in a blessed and abundant place of incredibly beautiful and diverse wildlife, nature messages or wild speak is so plentiful here.

Animals don't always need to present physically too, I feel like that is important to mention here. While I was pregnant with the twins I became obsessed with turtles, I would just draw them all the time. And would find turtle related things every where I went. It's super cute and ironic that my previous vision board had included two little identical turtles, because I really thought I would get pet turtles at that stage of my life. The universe delivered two little identical girls instead and I know the turtle connection was calling for me to slow down and enjoy sailing through life with these two little magical beings. Isn't it wild how all of the pieces of the puzzle come together, in the most unexpected ways.

Numerology

Another way the universe is always speaking to me is through numbers. Yes I'm one of those people who get excited when I see 11.11 and have an album full of screenshot angel numbers on my phone! Why? I don't know. I have been questioning that practice recently as my phone memory struggles with the weight of my habits! Once you start paying attention to numbers, you'll notice that they truly surround us. What better

Today is a Gift. That's why it's called the Present.

way to get important communication through? We encounter numbers every day, our phones, clocks, radios, computers. Seeing and understanding special number sequences is a beautiful way to maintain connection and communication with the universe that yes I am listening and I am hearing the guidance that you are sending. I have a very basic 'go-to' understanding of single digits and number sequences that I see regularly. For more unusual sequences or numbers that I don't connect with so often I have Doreen Virtue's "Angel Numbers 101" saved on my phone and I reference that regularly. I love the guidance, messages and reassurances that numbers offer. I consciously notice and connect with the numbers around me, specifically in times when I feel I need a little extra guidance or reassurance. As a simple reference I will share here some of my numerical messages. As always, I encourage you to explore and feel into numbers for yourself. What I share here is from my experience and years of connecting with their meanings, through synchronistic number flashes and numerology readings.

> 0 – A clean slate. A fresh page. A new chapter. Infinite potential. The need to let go.
>
> 1 – New beginnings. 11 – is a doorway, a gateway, a reminder to check in with myself and my alignment, to step through the door way into deeper alignment if that is what is required in that moment. 111 – the angels are with me. Manifesting potential amplified.
>
> 2 – Duality. Two sides to everything. Light and shadow.

3 – All that is. Everythingness. The holy trinity. The past, present, future. Mind, body, spirit. Head, heart, home.

4 – An encouraging nudge to keep going with my manifestations. I'm half way there.

5 – Manifesting potential is amplified. 555 – manifesting potential is amplified. Now is a time to check in with my mindset and my money stories.

6 – Check my external. Is it in alignment with my soul and higher purpose.

7 – Spiritual development. Express gratitude for all that is and for the infinite interconnectedness.

8 – Everything! Infinite potential. The link between heaven and earth. The bigger picture.

9 – Endings. Closing of chapters. An opportunity to tie up loose ends. 99 – what do I need to let go of.

I see numbers everywhere and often make decisions based on the numbers that present. If I am online shopping and while waiting on the cart to load get the last min 'maybe I shouldn't' guilts, if the cart loads with a significant number sequence, you can guarantee I am doing it! I have bought cars based on their number plate sequences; our most recent car purchase was 434 WHY. We had just sold our house and were changing our car to tow 'our soon to be ours' caravan, 4+3+4=11, that was enough for me. Every time I say those plates in those early days of 'what the actual F are we doing' I would remember my WHY! We were manifesting bigger things, that we couldn't see yet. We just needed to take the leap and trust. And our car reminded us that the universe had our back. I was so sad to lose those plates, our current plates are less aligned but I am manifesting a new car in the next year and I know those plates will be even more magical. When we bought our first home, our street number was 44. I wasn't even really interested in going to view that one but when hubby showed me the address, I agreed. As soon as we walked in I 'got that feeling' and I knew it was right for us. That street number was a sign that we were on track, that this was the right chapter of our manifesting story at that time but that it was not finite. 4 is only half way to 8!

I am so excited by and passionate about the signs from the universe I could go on and on for many more pages, instead I am going to encourage your personal exploration of the signs that present for you. Don't take anything for granted. There is no such thing as coincidence, only divinely orchestrated synchronicities. If you believe this, the magic of the world around you will begin to unfold in new and unexpected ways. I feel like one of my most common catch phrases is 'you can't make this stuff up'. When you align yourself with the frequency of magic, which is the frequency of the natural world around us, incredible opportunities present. It is not our job to know why these things happen or to try to rationalise them. But to connect with them and to allow them to rekindle the magic within us, each and every time.

Chapter 14

Space to manifest – minimalism

Aligning your space and spending with your energy and values!

In my experience there is a direct correlation between creating physical space and welcoming in abundance in my life. There is incredible power in clearing space, in decluttering, and in physically clearing and cleansing your living space. This has been an incredibly healing journey for me, not that I was ever a hoarder, but I was the kinds of person who held on to things for way too long, not realising the energetic impacts it was having.

You see, our things hold energy. That is why, I believe, that some things can hold such great sentimental value. But just as things can hold good energy, they can also hold less favourable energy or lack.

Clearing out our physical space

The joy and sense of freedom, or peace that I found when I began to give myself permission to let go of things that I had been holding on to, was absolutely incredible. As I write this I have a shipping container on the property we live on waiting for our attention, but after 2 years of not touching anything inside of there, I'm not sure what I will even be interested in holding on to once we do finally get around to opening those doors!! My minimalism journey began about 8 years ago when my niece introduced me to a podcast called 'The Minimalist'; I was instantly hooked. I was already an avid journaler; a practice I quickly dubbed, minimalism for my mind. And now I was armed and ready to take this decluttering into my physical realm. I began with my wardrobe as it felt like the easiest place for me to make quick and fast decisions. I had recently become a mum, my body had changed, my values had realigned and my life was never going to be the same again. So there was plenty in that closet that I was ready to part with. I began to work through each item of clothing, asking myself firstly if it still fit. Was it something I was going to wear with twin babies to care for; could I bend over comfortably, feed, etc? Was it comfortable (comfort was a priority for me then and that's a fashion realignment that I have held firm to since too!)? Did it suit my style? I had plenty of items in there from my corporate world and there was no way I was planning on returning to that grind any time soon!

Rapidly I noticed the freedom this new minimised wardrobe brought to my life. I was no longer overwhelmed by decisions and choices when getting dressed in the mornings and I had more space to play and create styles that suited my new lifestyle. One thing I did notice over time and I caution now when supporting people on their minimalist journey was that my capsule wardrobe quickly became boring. I had staples that were adaptable and great mix and match options but not much pattern or colour. Once I had that realisation I slowly added pieces that were more fun and vibrant again. As I grow and heal, my values and alignments change, as does my wardrobe. I clear out and add new items from the local op shop regularly, in an attempt to be more truly aligned with my expression of my inward self out into the world! This is something that is ever evolving and I know I have not found my style yet. I also know that an extreme minimalist, capsule wardrobe is not conducive to the more expressive version of self that I am cultivating. I've found happy ground somewhere in the middle!

Once I'd finished my wardrobe, I turned my attention to other areas of the house. Quickly learning that this is a never ending process. By the time I'd worked my way through each room or each area of my life, my values had realigned again and I was ready to let go of more. It was like a slow chip, even though every time felt like 'the big one', 'the one that would end all culls', but still they continue!!! I became more mindful of what was coming in and that eased the pressure of always wanting to cull, somewhat. Being mindful of what we bring in is something that I value and still am working on finessing. Gifts are a tricky one, and my abundant little manifestors, get lots of gifts! I've got them on board somewhat, especially with bigger items that are not aligned with our values as a family and I ask (them and myself, depending on the situation) is this something that we truly want, need and desire in our lives? Does it have a purpose and will it be used regularly to fill it's purpose? Does it align with our values (environmentally friendly, zero waste goals)? Where will it live?. It's not about not letting anything in, but it's about being discerning so that we don't end up drowning in a sea of 'stuff' again!

Rather than doing big culls now, I tend to do it as I go. I constantly have an 'op shop' bag on the go and anything that no longer feels aligned goes in there. While folding laundry if I notice that one of my little loves clothing's have holes or are too worn, they go straight in the bin. No second chances here! That eases the load when I do larger clear outs.

There is so much space and freedom in living with less. And I've found that the less we have the less we desire. It is a powerful cycle that takes us out of the consumer overspend, fast fashion pandemic. Our earth cannot sustain us if we continue to consume and discard as we do. I'll chat a bit more into this when I mention my zero waste mission that I'm currently learning.

Today is a Gift. That's why it's called the Present.

Tech tox!

This is one area of minimalism that I am always working on. Not just minimising the time I spend on my phone but also the distractions that my device contains. I've always been the type of person to be overwhelmed if I open my inbox and there are 100+ unread emails. I cannot deal with that level of 'to-do's' mulling around in the back of my mind. And so I am committed to regularly clearing my inbox, unsubscribing to anything that is no longer aligned and deleting spam. I am mindful to not keep out of date, misaligned or unused apps on my phone too, deleting anything that I don't use regularly. I regularly make time to delete or sort and file photos and notes on my phone too. What is the use of having all of these, in some cases 10s of 1000s of photos stored on our devices? I often find myself considering what will ever come of those photos, will our families every sit around a device and scroll through them the way we do with photo albums, or will they perpetually sit in my never ending, never coming to fruition 'to do' list waiting to be created into a printed photo book or similar! Who knows! All I know is, after committing to sorting and filing them more regularly, I am much more discerning about the photos I take now!

    Notifications are another element of my technology that I like to minimise. I remember the feeling of freedom and the sense of peace that came when I first turned off all of my notifications. It was delightful. Not only am I minimising the overwhelm that my phone was causing me, and eliminating the sense of urgency in checking it every time it dinged. But I am much more present as a result too. I only open my emails when I consciously choose to and when I have time to be present with their content. I do not check my messages until I have a moment to reply and respond fully present. Now I say this with so much confidence, I do need to be transparent here. This is a commitment that I ebb and flow with. My most recent addiction healing has been my phone and it is tougher and more focus consuming than I thought. Although the minimal notifications certainly do assist with this screen detox process, I still have some way to go. I took a big step on this tech tox free path and removed myself from social media. What a wild and wonderful thing to do in this day and age; when the world around us is so reliant and indeed addicted to it. I was addicted.

If you have a better relationship with social media than I do and indeed with your phone in general, good on you! I salute you, I truly do. This piece of the book was simply to share my experience and encourage reflection and an honest inventory of where you can minimise distractions in your life.

Zero Waste

This has been one wild ride. Gaining an understanding of just how wasteful I have been throughout my life was confronting and a challenge that I have realised requires a lot of commitment to overcome. We are so conditioned to not think of the consequences of our day-to-day lives, but the price to the earth is phenomenal. We are a society that creates catastrophic amounts of waste every single day and there's no sign of stopping. I used to think that I was just one person and I couldn't really make all that much difference.

Now I believe that if I can reduce this negative impact in any little way it is totally worth it. I have big goals with this, personal goals, on reducing my contribution to the worlds woeful waste significantly more and I take small consistent steps to walk more gently on the earth.

I need to do a full disclaimer here and add that I have been doing this dance for some time now, there have been huge leaps forward and some big steps back. I used to get so frustrated and self-critical and I can assure you that that is not the best approach. Allow yourself grace, we are unlearning some big habits here and a lifetime of conditioning that doesn't really reflect too much on the honesty of the impact our use of plastics has. My recent alignment with some local conservation groups has really inspired me and indeed, highlighted how much work I personally still have to do to reach my zero waste goal. Just don't forget, as I remind myself often, taking small steps can make a big difference and one step back doesn't mean you've failed, you can always try again. That applies to everything in life really right? If I've had a rough day with my children, I always ensure I finish the day with a reassurance that 'tomorrow is a new day and an opportunity for me to do better'.

My biggest inspiration in this zero waste journey has been Bea Johnson and, after listening to her speak in Brisbane some years ago, my commitment to integrating her teachings into my daily life is something that continues to grow. It is a massive topic and there are many facets to it. What I want to share here are the main drivers and tools that I lean on to assist me in my personal journey on zero waste living. My intention is to show you how it relates to my minimalism journey, for me they go hand in hand, and to hopefully inspire some more conscious action on your part. Perhaps you are already a zero waste king or queen, or maybe you haven't ever really given thought to the impact your daily habits have on this increasing issue. I hope that reading this chapter inspires some honest conversations and some conscious realignments. As I was writing this chapter I realised, I am likely adding this as an accountability partner for myself too. When my goal is out there, I have got to walk my talk in taking action to achieve it. Thanks for being my accountability partner by simply picking up this book. I am firmly in your cheer squad too.

One of my biggest goals with this (and an area that I am still working on) is conscious food sourcing and food shopping. We are so conditioned for convenience. I find myself, still, despite my awareness, picking up a plastic bag of apples at the super market. A slightly better option would be to bring my reusable bags and pick loose ones. Or an even better option would be to head to the local farm produce guy and buy some good ones that are plastic free. The same with all of the foods that I buy really, what I am ultimately looking to do is reduce packaging, buy in bulk where possible and to source locally grown organic food. I am having conversations and setting myself up for more mindful shopping, it will align divinely I know. Where I am at is exactly where I am meant to be and I have called in this wonderful community of growers and conscious consumers to inspire me and teach me their ways. One element of this zero waste goal that I am much better at honouring and achieving is saying no to fast fashion. I am an avid op shopper and for the most part incredibly aware of the fabrics I am buying from a micro plastics point of view. I love more natural fibres and consciously choose them as part of my zero waste goal. Fast fashion and cheap clothing not only contributes to our global landfill crisis but it is also not aligned with my values around 'slave labour' and equality. I love that the community that I live in are very like minded and there are no remarks passed if you wear the same outfit to every special event. That fast fashion mindset just hasn't penetrated here and I don't think I've ever heard an underhanded comment about what anyone is wearing. The only comments I here is 'I really love when you wear that dress' or 'that colour is so fab on you'. I have my girls on to this too, we love to up cycle clothing and play around with home done alterations and quirky additions to recycle things instead of throwing them out.

While makeup and skin care are not things that I really put much focus on or indeed effort in to, I do have some goals around this too for the odd occasion I decide to 'put my face on' as they say at home. Currently I try to shop consciously when buying cosmetics, I use natural skin care; usually only coconut oil or castor oil for pretty much everything! Hair care is a little more tricky for me, being a curly girl I've yet to find a super effective low tox, low waste solution, but I do have a friend on the case.

In a nutshell, this is the Bea Johnson 5 steps that I try to be mindful of as I take action to reduce my waste contribution to the world.

1. Refuse (what we do not need)

This for me was a learning curve. And is still a work in progress. Learning to say no as someone who has always been a yes person was weird. Also, it goes against what I say about money manifesting. But incoming 'clutter' or misaligned items are not abundance, they are distraction! I began by practising saying no to things that felt easy for me; the bag at the super market, the receipt at the shop, the napkins at the cafe or the disposable chopsticks at the sushi shop. Then I flexed it with things that felt a bit more tricky for me; free goody bags at the fairs, merch at community engagement days, etc. if it is not useful to me, in alignment with my values or my goals, then it is not necessary. This is a little trickier with my little loves but we are working on it.

2. Reduce (what we do need and cannot refuse)

There are things that are a little more difficult to refuse or to be without. I think a good example of this for me is plastic bowls, plates, cups and cutlery for my little loves. I trialled the glass thing and there were too many breaks, extra messes to clean and band aids to administer! They are just too young. So now, they have one each and we use them until their end of life. No seasonal changes or new fad following, we care for them well so they last longer and get as much use as possible out of each item.

Today is a Gift. That's why it's called the Present.

3. Reuse (what we consume and cannot refuse or reduce)

Op-shopping! As if I needed another excuse. No though seriously, I have become so much better at this with practice. I used to go in there and all kinds of persona's would wash over me. No Claire! That white dress is not suitable for block living with three very attached grubby handed little loves!!! Now I never compromised on fabric, fit or colour. If it is not something I would pay full price for, it does not come home with me just because it's only $3!!!. There is an art to it and it has taken many years of practice! I can't say I'm fully there, but much improved!

More examples of this too are re-purposing things that you have already used; that coffee jar is perfect for bulk dry food items. The old t-shirt a rag. Fabric square a beeswax wrap. The potential for reusing is so much bigger than we initially see. Allow yourself to expand your thinking and get creative. This part can be particularly fun.

4. Recycle (what we cannot refuse, reduce or reuse)

Recycling can be a mine field depending on your location and local recycling policies. It is good to educate yourself on that and to see what steps you can take. This is one that I am particularly bad at. Since moving I haven't really gotten into the flow of this and have yet to do my research. At our old house, I had local council signs up next to the bins to guide us and we were making much more headway with step one and two so this was greatly reduced too. This is certainly one area that I am devoted to improving in the coming months.

5. Rot (Compost the rest)

We compost as much as we can and give as much fruit and veg my family eat that's quite a bit. Composting has so many benefits, not just to reducing our waste footprint but also can be a very rewarding part of an intentional gardening process.

Essentially zero waste is about living more mindfully and simplifying our lives. I know that will sound like a complete oxymoron if you are brand new to this, trust me it did to me too. How does having to change all of your habits around shopping, plastic and waste equal simplicity? I do not deny these changes can feel big, complex and complicated to start with, quite the opposite of simple. But trust me, once you find your flow and begin to make the changes, life becomes much simpler. Everything is connected right. So once you have found flow with these pivots, you will be at least open to pivoting in area's of your life you never thought you would pivot before.

Chapter 15

Scheduling – Perimeters for the pivot

Something that, when initially suggested to me felt quiet the opposite to the pivot that I pride myself on, was scheduling. When my conscious parenting coach suggested that I would benefit from introducing a schedule to my life, to assist my quest to be more present in all the things that are constantly calling my attention, I could literally feel the resistance arise in my body. Was she serious? Had she missed the memo in our earlier sessions where I spoke into my desire to be more of a 'go with the flow' kind of mum, who could be present and relax. My thoughts around scheduling were rigid, harsh and well, to be honest, restrictive. I just couldn't see how it was going to work for me. I am all about the pivot and I just didn't see how these two 'polarities' could go hand *in hand. Most of you know, I am a homeschooling mama, soul led business owner, trying to be as present as I can for my husband, my children and my wonderful village of friends, my work, my study, my health, my well-being all of the things!!! How was putting myself into a 'boxish' schedule going to help? She could obviously feel the shift in my energy, the racing in my mind and the fear in my nervous system. She gently encouraged me to just give it a go, I had nothing to lose right!*

I printed the template and got to work!

Firstly, I allowed myself to get intentional about why I was doing this process in the first place. I got super clear on my intentions and my desired outcome. I began to write a list of the things that I wanted to prioritise in my week. My list looked something like this:

- ~ homeschooling activities
- ~ family adventures
- ~ date night with my husband
- ~ social time with our friends
- ~ time out for myself
- ~ play time with my little wild ones
- ~ reading time
- ~ work / study time
- ~ free time / down time
- ~ rest / home days
- ~ Home making
- ~ Cleaning
- ~ Laundry
- ~ meditation
- ~ yoga

Today is a Gift. That's why it's called the Present.

I'm not going to lie, I was feeling incredibly overwhelmed. How on earth was I planning to get all of that scheduled in to one weekly schedule. It was like a self-fulfilling prophecy, my mind confirmed the fears 'this really was going to be impossible', 'I truly do need a clone'! I almost gave up at the first hurdle, there was just too much. I took a moment, took a breath and then started with the things that I knew. I first added our current commitments; classes, weekly events etc.

Mornings in our place are very dependant on how the night before has flowed (sleepless little wildlings make for a tired mama some mornings) so I knew my mornings needed to be flexible and expectation free. So rather than lock myself into anything in the first slot every day I wrote 'Morning Rhythms', that gave me the flexibility I needed. On the back of the schedule I listed how my ideal morning looks (oral health rituals, morning yoga, journaling, meditation, breath work, breakfast, morning tidy up) that way I have an anchor if we are tired and I need some inspiration or direction. But it doesn't feel locked in for me. If my morning only allows for a couple of those items, I can try to fit the rest in to moments later in the day! That is the key to this scheduling thing; to find flow and flexibility within the framework!

I did the same in the evening time slot for our evening rhythms, we love dinner with friends and have dinner out of home often so having a strict evening routine wouldn't work for us. My evening rhythms list looks something like (dinner, evening tidy up, family connection time, daily reflections and gratitude, bedtime routines) these flow as simply as our mornings do.

From there, I worked through my list focusing on things that needed a daily time slot. And then began to see how this could all flow together. It took some time and devotion to the task but as it came together more and more, I felt the restrictiveness I'd initially been overtaken by, lessen and lessen.

What I ended up with was a really clear visual of how, with a little bit of self discipline (boundaries is something I am still working on) I really could find time in my week for all of the things that my soul desired! The feelings that were so overwhelming in the early stages of this suggestion had transcended into an empowered excitement. Suddenly, I felt very capable and happy that so many things that had been neglected through lack of organisation and boundaries with myself could have their place in my heart full days.

What I also learned as I got further into this flow was that flexibility was much easier (for me) when there was a perimeter. I realised quickly that not only could my plans change and could I still pivot, in truth, the pivot was less overwhelming than ever before because now I had a visual to see what was being 'parked in the pivot'. For example, if my friend needed something on a Tuesday afternoon, unexpected visitors arrived, or an unplanned appointment popped up or an opportunity for something great instead of just dismissing my regular Tuesday rhythms or allowing them to fall away, I had a clear visual of what was being 'sacrificed' and an ability to find time and space for that later in the week. I could much more easily park an activity,

Today is a Gift. That's why it's called the Present.

knowing I would swap it's time slot out than just allow it to fall away into the spiral of overwhelm that were unattended tasks in my mind.

Some days emotions or energetics within our family would mean that I am required to be more present with the children during the day. If my work and study time needed to be altered, I could decide what was a bigger priority for me that evening. What was scheduled? Or what had been parked? Making sure that I found time for the other later in the week.

One of the greatest gifts from this process for me has been the quietening of my monkey mind. When that mind chatter of 'I should be doing something else' comes in, usually telling me I should be working while I'm playing with the children, or that I should be playing with the children while I'm working, I have been much more equipped to quieten it quickly. Knowing that where ever it is trying to redirect my focus has it's own place on my schedule. Being full present in my work for example allows me to be more productive, my little loves are way more accepting of a small burst of work because their cups are already filled or they know that a family adventure is following. Being fully present with my family fosters more quality time and secure relationships. And dedicated time to write means my creativity and passion is not 'suffering' due to other priorities. This way everything has it's time and place and I can guilt free indulge myself fully present in that task at hand!

I can almost feel the resistance in some of you, if you've not done this before, it can be hard, I get it! But like me in those early days when it was suggested for me, you have nothing to loose. Just give it a go!

This was a version of mine while I was writing this chapter of the book. It's interesting to see how much it has shifted again. I allow myself to review my schedule often to ensure that it is continuing to serve us as best it can.

	MON	TUE	WED	THUR	FRI	SAT	SUN
7-9am	MR	MR	MR	MR	MR	MR	MR
9-11am	Laundry Life Admin	Home school Beach hangs	Play w/ WO House/ work	Outing (park / skate / ride)	Home Make / block		Family Adventure
11-1pm	Home school Lunch	Beach Hangs Lunch	Home school Lunch	Read write Lunch			
1-3pm	Free time	CREATE w/Wild Ones	Dinner prep Work / Study	Free time	Social Friend time		
3-5pm	Dinner prep Mama Me Time	Read / Write	Family walk Play w/ WO			Mama Me Time	
5-7pm	ER	ER	ER	ER	ER	ER	ER
7-9pm	Work	Date Night	Read / Write	Study / Rest	Free	Read	Date Night

Remember, this is a journey! Your schedule will change. You are the author, you can re-write this thing as many times as you need to! PLAY with it, make it work for you!

Today is a Gift. That's why it's called the Present.

Infusing your days of the week with some extra magic!

Something I like to be mindful of when creating my schedule are the magical associations for each day. This isn't something I can always stick to but where I can, I consider this while scheduling.

Monday – Cleansing and Healing.

I usually use Monday as my reset day. We usually have busy weekends so Monday is about slowing down, connecting with my intuition, following my own flow, cooking nourishing food and nurturing my beautiful home.

Tuesday – Action, Power and Success.

Tuesdays are wonderful days for getting stuff done. I believe Tuesdays energy is also very masculine so I tend to do more hands on activities on that day. This is also my preferred day to tend to things like the car and outdoor chores.

Wednesday – Communication, Community and Knowledge.

I love that our local home-school meet up is on a Wednesday, I feel like it is a perfect day for it. It is also a great day for study, manifesting, business, money and good luck. If you are a writer or an aspiring writer, Wednesday is a great day to create your magic!

Thursday – Growth and Good Luck.

Thursday is another great day for all things business, progress, and manifesting. I feel like it is the action steps of Wednesday's more creative flow. Thursday is a great day to focus on abundance and your career.

Friday – Love, Friendship, Creativity.

Friday is a day for beauty, for flow, friendship and nurturing your most important relationships. Isn't it funny how we so intuitively do these things. Friday used to be date night for us, now it is a regular beach dinner with friends. All intuitively guided.

Saturday – Protection, Cleansing, Routine.

Who else always had a solid Saturday morning cleaning routine growing up. Turns out it was more than just convenient timing at the end of the busy week. It is a powerful time for cleaning and cleansing. It is also a great day for self discipline and start new healthy habits and routines.

Sunday – Empowerment and Joy.

Sunday is such a powerhouse day; I absolutely love it. I use it as my anchor for some serious self care and will try, most weeks, to honour myself with a little indulgence, a face mask, a foot bath, something along those lines. Sundays are also powerful days for personal growth, creativity and healing. Anything that brings you joy and sparks your soul. I use the success energy of Sunday to set me up for the week ahead; reviewing our schedule, getting organised (even if it's just mentally – I do the more logistical, practical organisation on a Monday!) setting my self up to thrive.

Each week I review my schedule and ensure that there are no changes. I also consider any additional rituals or regular rhythms that may be present in that week. For example if it is the start or the end of a month, a full or new moon, or any other significant observation or celebration day on our calendar.

Regular Rituals

I am going to share here a snap shot of some of the regular rituals that I include to enhance my schedule, magic and flow!

Each week on a Sunday I make time to reflect on the week that's been; I allow myself an honest opportunity to see what has unfolded, what I would like to celebrate, change, express gratitude for. This is also when I review the schedule for the week ahead and make any changes.

At the start of a new calendar month, I make time to sit with and review my goals. Are they still in alignment? Are there any changes to be made? Am I focused and do I know what action is required from me this month?

At the end of the calendar month, I take time to review the month that has been. Much like my weekly review but a bit bigger scale. How are my goals tracking? Did I take the action I'd intended to etc?

With each full moon, I take the opportunity to sit with my journal and let go of any challenges, struggles or misaligned energies. My favourite full moon rituals include; journaling and letting go, a fire ceremony where I burn the journaled pages if I feel called to, otherwise I simply fire gaze. I charge my crystals and sit under the moon and admire her beauty.

With each New Moon, I make time to sit with my intentions, to review them and to set new ones for the month ahead. I celebrate what I have achieved in the month past and I allow myself to visualise the month ahead and all that I intend to create in my reality. My other favourite new moon rituals include cleaning and cleansing my home and car, taking a relaxing and revitalising new moon bath, creating an altar for the month ahead.

At the start of every season, I take time to connect in with the energy of that season and what it will potentially mean for me and my journey.

At the end of every season, I sit again in reflection. How did that play out? What did I learn? What am I grateful for etc.

At the end of every year (I do new year a few times for different things – calendar year, astrological year and my birth year!) I reflect and review, then I visualise and look ahead getting myself into the vibration of what it is that I am creating and calling in.

I love including wholesome ritual into my daily rhythm. My beautiful friend and mentor Dania Foster says 'a ritual is something that is done with reverence over and over again'. Writing this book was a ritual in itself. I had my little tool kit that I would bring with me and use each time I connected with this content. One afternoon my daughter sat next to me while I was writing and told me she liked my set up. It's cute! I have a couple of cards that have been with me since the first day I sat to finally get this book together, two crystals, clear quartz and moonstone, a cute little beeswax candle that my little loves hand-rolled and an essential oil roller that a dear friend gifted me, the box said 'oil blend for flow' and instantly I knew it's purpose in my life. (While writing this book, I have it saved as my laptop as 'finding flow' awaiting it's final name to drop in!) It's all stored in a cute colourful little bag that I carry with me where ever I decide to go to write.

You might notice that there is a lot of time for reflection and introspection in my schedule and regular rituals. I feel that it is important to explore that a little further here. Our busy lifestyles so often keep us disconnected, even from ourselves. We tend to be disconnected from our experience and our learnings as we journey through our days. A lesson or a challenge arises and we navigate it, moving on without much thought or consideration for the speed bump that presented or why. Reflection and introspection are essential ingredients in this growth potion and if we are to heal and transcend, we must not be afraid to see the truth of ourselves, where we are at, and the experiences that we are calling in. There is no hiding here. Remember if you are going to take the helm as the captain of this ship, you must be fully aware of your crew and the sailing conditions. Often times people are afraid to reflect or to go inward because they are afraid of or challenged by what they will see. Do not be afraid, be brave! You've got this.

The future is yours,

Write it well.

Chapter 16

Write Your Story Strong!

When we are wildly aware of our thoughts, actions and even our words, we are truly stepping up in taking responsibility for where we are at and the direction that we are steering this ship! I've always loved the power of words and have been playing magical word games since as long as I can remember. Recently in my studies with Tyler Tolman he discussed "Relationshits and Relationships" and I couldn't love it anymore. In this chapter, we are focusing a lot on our relationSHIP with words... making a conscious decision to limit the shit!

The more aware of that we are with our words, the more focused on our vision (we will cover this in the next chapter), the more present, the more grateful, the more powerful our manifesting magic becomes. The spells that we cast in every moment (even the silent ones – the thoughts in our head) contribute to this manifestation process. And that is why awareness and self accountability are so important. We cast spells every single day. When we affirm that we are healthy, tired, stressed, happy, so it is. Understanding the power of the words we use, can not only assist us in staying more focused on what we desire or assist us in maintaining the higher vibrations, but it also assists us greatly in communicating with the universe what it is that we are calling in.

There are so many wonderful resources and writings to explore around our complex relationship with language and I encourage you to delve into that world of learning if you feel called. What I choose to speak into here, are the resources that I return to time and time again to ensure that I am keeping myself in check and my words in alignment. Disclaimer – it's funny, I always get nervous writing about this. It's like my use of language is under a spotlight!! If you notice any discrepancies between what I'm saying and what I'm saying... feel free to remind me!

What I share below is a snap shot of my learnings around language and some of my favourite resources.

The Four Gates of Speech

Is it true? Is it necessary? Is it beneficial? Is it kind?

Imagine a world where we all passed our words through these gates before they were spoken. How very different life would be. It feels like the world in which we live, where words are used in absolute unnecessary excess, that our regard for language gets

The future is yours. Write it well.

more and more lost in its overuse! One of the biggest illuminations for me has been around the first gate... is it true? So many words have been lost in translation, either through totally human lack of regard, or through our societal conditioning. The reverence of the word and the sacredity (I may be making up words now... timely right!!!) of our spells diminishing all the time. When we even think of the term 'you have my word', how fickle has that become?

The power of our language and our connection to it is getting further out of our grasp with the increase in AI and more widespread use of it in everyday situations. I know as a poor speller, I was grateful for predictive text and spell checker. Soon we won't even have to think about how to string a sentence together, we will simply utter random words to our chat bots and allow them to create conversations for us!!!

This is a rabbit warren, that I didn't intend to enter, but I will say... It's an incredible curve in our learning that requires regular deep conversation, many open minds and reverence for the power of more deeply understanding our day-to-day language. This is the stuff that makes my soul sing and conversing on such topics truly brings us into deeper alignment and raises our vibrational energy, tenfold.

The Four Agreements

Another of my favourite tools is The Four Agreements. The first agreement relates directly to language and our use of it. 'Be impeccable with your word', I remember when I first read this how confronting and challenging it was for me. Hmmm... instantly I was in shame and guilt and aware of the work I had to do around this. One of my husband's pet hates, in our digital age, is our lack of regard with our word. He always muses that back in the day, when you said you would meet your mate at the shop at 10am, you would be there at 10am. There was no convenient way of letting them know that you were running 15 minutes late and so you made sure that you were on time. The four agreements is a book that I absolutely recommend that every human read at least annually. It is a powerful tool to assist us in living in alignment and keeping us accountable on our path to living our best life.

Melodic Mantra's

A powerful healing use of word is melodic mantras. We know the power and magic of mantra's and affirmations, adding melody takes them to the next level. I was introduced to chanting meditation a few years ago and truly fell in love. We practice Kirtan regularly and really notice a shift in our vibrational energy and indeed the energy of our home if we miss it for a while. Our brain to voice connection is so deep and profound, and when we feel into the difference that singing a mantra can make you instantly notice a shift. Allison Davies does wonderful work around teaching more about the science behind this and the power of music in healing. My favourite melodic mantra from her, is one I lean on often. As soon as there is as much as a sniffle in our home, I work with my body to affirm and reaffirm, over and over again 'every little cell in my body is happy', I encourage you if you are

The future is yours. Write it well.

keen to connect more with this to check out her work. If you are open to a chanting and Kirtan meditation recommendation, I encourage you to check out The Mantra Room, Brisbane (in person or on YouTube) or Edo & Jo on Spotify. These are my go-to's and although Brisbane is quite a journey for us now, every time we visit we do our best to fit in at least one visit to our beloved Kirtan group.

Affirmations

Our mindset is one of the greatest allies and biggest enemies we have in this journey of life. Trust me, I've danced with both sides. While my mindset is my enemy, flow is hard to find. Knowing that dark thoughts or negative self-talk are signs or symptoms of healing that is ready to surface is a powerful insight to have. I see our mind like a toddler, it is powerful and knows what it wants but sometimes the communication gets warped and so when we can approach it with love, kindness and a willingness to help, surrender is easier. I shared the story above about consciously creating our first thought in the morning, now lets look at what other mindset tools we can lean into as our days flow on. Affirmations are one powerful mindset buddy that is easy and we can take anywhere. I use affirmations and anchors which I will speak into in a moment to assist with building new habits or creating new behaviours for myself. I allow myself to think of an affirmation, to speak it, to feel it, to know it, to create it, to be it! There is that embodiment piece again. Affirmations are powerful and the more we use them the more easily embodied they become.

When I first started using affirmations I used to say 'I am building a successful business' and my friend pulled me up questioning when I was going to have 'built' it. At what point would my affirmation change or was I intending to build this business for ever. Where was my marker of success, when I sat with that and reflected, I realised that 'I enjoy success in my business' was a better and more adaptable fit for me. As a busy mama, homeschooling my little loves, continually 'building' was creating burn out and it was a moving goal post. I needed to affirm the success, now, in the moment.

"Our words are spells, that is why we call it spelling". Unknown.

My Journey with Changing My Language

Remember it is the simple changes, allowing ourselves time and space to connect with and reflect on the words that we use often that can have a profound impact. Understanding our personal relationship with certain words is a great insight into the energy we are creating each time we interact with those words. My daughter just recently started to ask me what my favourite words are, on her own reflection of her having favourite words. Hers were super cute and to an outsider not really significant to anything in particular or not of any importance, but she liked the sound of them. She likes the flow and the tone.

The future is yours. Write it well.

I liked that she has such awareness of the power of our human language at such a young age! I have been playing with words for as long as I can remember and am so grateful to see my little wildlings brain working in that way too.

Even my previous business tag line was a powerful word play MAKE EVERYDAY MAGIC... the reader can decide how to connect with that in each moment. Are we MAKING EVERY DAY MAGIC or EVERYDAY magic? There is no right or wrong, it simply is! Now let's have a look at some of my favourite word plays and swaps! Pay attention to your language, to your relationship with words over the next week or so and see what arises for you.

Release. When this word was broken down for me, I was mind-blown! When we re-lease something, we are telling the universe that we would like to re take the lease on that thing. I've replaced that word with let go.

I'm sorry. This is one that I am certainly still integrating. I'm sorry, stems from lack and makes it sound like we have done something wrong. Not to mention it is way overused and under-meant! (ha-ha another made up word... I do that a lot!!!) Instead of saying sorry, re frame it and focus on the positive. Swap out 'Sorry I'm late' or 'Sorry for the delay' to 'Thank you for your patience'. I challenge you to only say sorry when you REALLY mean it!

Discipline. This instantly gets my back up and sparks the retaliation or rebel in me! Discipline just by its very definition feels hard so I've been swapping it out for devotion or dedication, both feel much more sacred to me. I believe they come from a place of love not fear.

Nervous. I remember our oldest daughter speaking into her nerves before a performance once and her beautiful uncle encouraging her to re-frame her mind on that. What are you feeling he asked? She explained the butterflies in her tummy and he reminded her that the feeling is similar when we feel excited. Nerves and excitement are one and the same. Which feels better to you?

Breakfast. This one feels so obvious but after recently learning more about fasting and breaking a fast it changed drastically for me. When doing a fast, it is strongly encouraged to break it gently, to wake your digestive system up tenderly. Truly we break our fast every morning. When I began to re frame that word for myself my relationship with what I break my fast with shifted too. Our bodies can't optimally process heavy foods or caffeine loaded drinks first thing in the morning. This more gentle approach has played a huge role in a more gentle approach to so much more throughout my day too.

Should. A very dear friend of mine says 'If I'm saying I should, that almost certainly means I should not'. Should is so conditional and it very often takes us out of our aligned flow. If we are doing something because we 'should', on reflection we will usually find that it doesn't serve us well. Next time you feel yourself in a 'should' situation, ask yourself why? If it is aligned for you and feels good with your values, then go right ahead. If it's not, then reconsider a suitable alternative. Or at least review your wording! Should is almost

The future is yours. Write it well.

always a fear-based alignment, you've got the tools to work on that.

Can't. This is one that I banned from our household when our children were young. There is no such things as can't, we may not have the skills required for a certain task in that moment, but if we desire to, then we almost certainly can acquire them! We are manifesting powerhouses, yes? Nothing is off limits!!! Next time you experience a can't, whether it be yourself or in conversation with someone else, question it! Can't is such a lack mindset and keeps us in the lower vibrations, that is not where our manifesting magic happens with ease!

Try. You never try, you do! This is another word that there I say there is no such thing as. You either do or your don't. As someone who 'tried' a lot in the past, in hindsight, I realise how trying that was!!! Sorry, I couldn't help myself!!! Try is such a half-assed energy, you are either committed to doing, or you are not. If you are using try in the context of being uncertain of your abilities, try switching out for 'intention'. A personal example of this swap out – "I am going to try to fire twirl" to "my intention is to fire twirl by the end of this year!" This is one that still sneaks into my vocabulary often and even catches me by surprise.

This isn't about creating another thing that we can be super strict or harsh on ourselves about. It is simply about increasing our awareness and taking steps to bring our language into deeper alignment. The magic lies in being mindful and consciously correcting thoughts and words as we need to. I swear when I started this element of the work I would say "I take that back Universe, what I meant to say was...." 100 times a day! It was a little confronting to bring to my awareness just how negative and full of lack my language had been for so long. We are all partial to negative self-talk from time to time, you know how reaffirming that negative voice is in our mind when we get stuck in those loops, right? Well just like that persistence, these language shifts require consistence too... we are creatures of habit... repetition is key.

Another powerful example of how we can misuse language, mindlessly, is when I was making a conscious commitment to live a healthier lifestyle with regard to the food we were eating. For the most part I was doing great; we were making great progress with dietary changes but every now and then I would award us a 'treat'. What I didn't see initially was that my wording around these often sugar filled 'treats' was making them more desirable and building them to be somewhat special. But they weren't special. They were misaligned, as was my language! I began to shift the use of that word to delicious seasonal fruit that we really enjoyed. The punnet of lusciously red strawberries, the juicy mangos, it didn't take long at all until our focus was completely realigned. Our words were incredibly powerful in that process. Now we call chocolates etc, sugar. Because essentially that is mostly what they are, it helps us to be more conscious and aware of the choices that we are making around what we are putting into our bodies.

On reflection of my recent social media detox, I noticed so much new insight about the language we use there. Another interesting observation since exiting my zombie media state is the language that I hadn't even really ever questioned before. Language is something I love and there is a whole chapter dedicated to it later in the book, but for the sake of this musing I want to share a few of the most challenging words that have entered a new state of awareness for me. Followers: it's no wonder our world is saturated with self entitled 'god complex' leaders! When creating content for their 'followers'. The word and idea of that creates an image of hierarchical set up in my mind and that is something that my spirit naturally dispels. It just feels so wrong on every level. Strengthening the divide. Likes; I have been in that trap more than once where my self confidence held taut on the tightrope of external validation as I checked (every few minutes) the likes on a post. What is actually with that?? Not enough "Likes" drives a message home that we are not good enough, not 'liked', to a self critical person that can be detrimental. Although my relationship with numbers and likes has been radically different in recent years, this realisation reinforced the idea that I was parting ways with social media as one of the biggest commitments I have ever made to my mental health. Feed; we don't see it but we are literally 'feeding' our brain (and our internal stories) with the content that we consume on social media. As someone who was very conscious of what was on my feed I thought I was somewhat immune to this one. But on deeper reflection I realised that I was subconsciously comparing myself to my content, whether I liked it or not. That homeschooling mum is way more creative than me, that friend is so much more adventurous, that influencer prettier, I did not realise it but my self confidence was shot! I was questioning myself in things that I am usually so confident with and negatively reaffirming to myself constantly that I simply wasn't enough. It was only with a break from it that I could see if for what it was. And finally reels; I'm not going to harp on too much more, I know you all get the point. This one, I couldn't leave out. If I were playing a word game where I had to think of the first thing that came to mind when I heard the word reel, my mind would instantly go to fishing! You reel in a fish, with your hook! Well I was caught alright; hook, line and sinker!

Chapter 17

Make the Next One Your Best Chapter Yet!

Like many aspects of this journey, when I was first introduced to the concept of writing a vision, I was feeling incredibly overwhelmed. I was at a stage in my life where things were not flowing quite in the way I'd intended. What I've come to learn as misalignment; the moment seemed so out of control and so far out of my reach that I didn't have a vision for the next 5 days never mind the future. So it is my intention in sharing this with you to offer it simply, to break it down into manageable chunks and to encourage you to meet yourself where you are at. That is truly the only place to start!

The first vision I created was so clunky and much editing was required. Since then, over the many years of use, I have adapted my process somewhat to fit more authentically with my personal flow and the regular rhythms. I share this practiced and adapted version with you here. There will be many variations of this out there in the world, and as always, I encourage you to play with it and find a flow that feels right for you.

Essentially, this vision is the story which we are co-creating with the universe. It is written in the present tense with mindful use of words and language, evoking the higher frequency energies to bring us into vibrational match of that with which we are manifesting.

At the time of writing my first vision, my twin girls were very young and we were all adjusting to our new, radically different family dynamic. As well as the usual new mum fears around keeping these new tiny humans alive, I found myself wrapped up in an additional layer of fear. Worry that my bonus daughter, not mine by birth, would feel abandoned or less loved now that her tiny little siblings was taking so much of my focus, attention and energy... oh the energy! The sleeplessness was real! Upon hearing that we were expecting twins, a fellow twin mum friend had mused that I wouldn't sleep again for at least four years... we're past eight now and counting!!! I've long since forgotten much of that first vision but the opening line is a mantra that I still recall and feel as clear as the day I wrote it. Indeed I still lean on these words, although now it has been adapted to include our son too. "I am a loving, caring and nurturing mother to three beautiful girls". I would recite that line, and my full vision, multiple times a day. In those early mothering days I would recite this mantra when I felt challenged, overwhelmed, frustrated or felt doubt in my ability. This became a powerful tool of energy realignment any time that my thoughts, words or actions were feeling out of alignment with my favourite version of self.

For me, a most effective and efficient vision has a holistic approach. It is detailed, emotive but also short and to the point. We certainly don't want it to be too long or the process of connecting with it daily can become arduous and unattainable. I keep mine to a maximum of one page in my journal and I re-write it every morning. I love that I am writing this part of my book on New Years Eve and I have a fresh vision to start of the new calendar year tomorrow morning. I created it in an inspired moment a few days ago and have been tweaking and revising it as I need to. I know that it will continue to evolve as I connect more deeply with it. My intention is to write it out every day, at least once, until it undoubtedly becomes my reality.

Writing it out is an important part of the process but I mentioned above that it needs to be emotive. That is to help us embody the vibrational frequency of the future that we are calling in. it's all well and good to think it, to say it, but when we feel it, truly feel it, that is where the magic absolutely lies. I encourage you to practice this, tweak and make your vision feel great in your body. Every morning you are seeing it, feeling it, calling it in and strongly visualising it. There is so much that I want to speak into here around inspired action and how desiring something is simply just not enough. Affirming you want more of something will not necessarily mean that the universal delivery system will load their truck and deliver it right to you. Instead, it might come through a sequence of inspired actions that lead you to the 'pick up' dock of your desired outcome instead.

And understanding the power and magic of divine timing is important here too. Sometimes our universal cart checkout may experience some delays, perhaps there are steps to be taken before we can be fully in the frequency of matching what we are calling in. Or there will be some other divinely orchestrated delay. Another opportunity or reminder to surrender. I often find that when there is a significant delay, my desire is not truly in alignment. I've missed a piece of the puzzle or on deep introspection and reflection I can see that I am simply required to pivot slightly or to slow down. Divine delays, in my experience, often present when I am rushing or pushing and not surrendering to the flow.

So how do I even begin to create my vision? Sometimes it is as simple as sitting down, writing out my desires and allowing it to flow. Other times I need a little more guidance, structure or prompting. In those cases I return to my wheel of wellness or my intentions list from Chapter 3 and I work through each section [health, career, biz, life purpose, finances, family, close relationships, friends, community, personal joy, fun, hobbies, growth, study, physical environment, spirituality] feeling into what it is that I truly desire, noting what presents in each area. From there I write my vision, I prefer to write it in paragraph form but some people prefer a list or affirmation style, whatever resonates with you is most important. The reason that I encourage people, especially if you are new to this work, to use the categories above is to ensure that you are incorporating a holistic approach. What can sometimes happen, in my experience and what I have witnessed with others, is that often times we can become more focused on one area of life while unconsciously neglecting another. I was often guilty of having a very clear vision for my career and becoming hyper focused on that, negating any growth or healing in my family or home areas. This is all about aligning with our favourite version of self, right? So surely, when we truly feel into it, our favourite version of self is a well-rounded person?

Your vision should be something that creates joy and excitement within you, it should spark enthusiasm. The same is true if we are more visual creatives and prefer to use a more visually pleasing vision board or dream board. Oh man, how I love those things. Just recently I was reflecting on one of my most powerful ones. I created this vision board early in my relationship with my husband. I was holding a workshop and his sister was in attendance. I didn't want to scare anyone off or seem too pushy so I decided to omit the beautiful image of an engagement ring that I had cut out of a magazine, there was plenty of time to add that to a later board! On that vision board, I remember including a picture of two little turtles (I've shared this story in another section of the book I am sure!), the words 'permanent Australian visa', a picture of a beautiful doggy, among other things. I followed the usual steps of vision board manifesting and placed it in my bedroom, each morning on rising, I would connect with that board and feel all of the excitement and anticipation of these dreams being manifested into my reality. One by one, as these dreams were realised or delivered, their corresponding piece on the board would synchronistically 'lose its stick' and fall off! I noticed this most when the two turtles fell off a day or so before finding out that my growing belly was nurturing twins. You actually can't make this stuff up!!! Every element of that vision board came to pass and just reflecting on that I can feel all of the feels I felt as each one did. Reconnecting with that memory truly still sparks a drive deep within me to recreate a vision board as powerful again. Perhaps that is something I will do in the coming weeks, once this book is off being proof read.

I referenced the engagement ring that I'd decided not to add. Years later, while the pieces of the puzzle were falling into place (and off my vision board!) I was cleaning out some boxes with my then fiance when we happened across the box of vision board creating supplies. We found the picture of the ring and I kid you not, it was almost identical to the one that my now husband had placed on my hand only months before. When creating a vision board, I encourage you to be as specific and as focused as you can. If you desire a white car, do not add a picture of a red one, even if it is exactly the same model etc. Unless of course you are willing to compromise on the colour. It is like you are filling in an order form with the universe, nine times out of ten, it is going to be delivered, exactly how you ordered it!

Chapter 18

Money Manifesting

"Money is a tool, not the goal, freedom is the goal. Don't forget that." Bob Proctor

My journey with money manifesting has been so deeply healing and so profound, that I couldn't not dedicate a fully chapter to this in it's own right. Coming to the understanding that money is energy was one of the biggest and most powerful learnings for me on this journey. Energy, I understand; I've been playing in this realm for a long time. Finances I didn't. I grew up with a subconscious belief that only rich people really understood money and that people like me could never learn 'the secrets'. No money magic for me, I must work hard and mind my pennies. My life experiences seemed to confirm that. Lack, struggle, poor choices and debt! Lots of debt! What an absolutely welcome relief it was to dig into, heal and rewrite these stories for myself. Remembering the basic 101 where our focus goes our energy flows. I realise now that I was so focused on debt, my fear of it mounting, with my interest! I couldn't answer private number phone calls and I had all but accepted that this would be my lot in life. I felt helpless and could see no way out. Now, I do want to add a disclaimer here, my debt was relatively small in the debt consumed world that we live in but the misaligned energy it created within me told me it was wrong for me, even if I didn't understand how or why yet! A series of synchronistic events brought money manifesting to the forefront of my healing journey, as it does. I always say the universe delivers exactly what we need at exactly the right time and at that time I needed help to heal and to find the freedom to breathe fully and confidently again. And so it came in the form of synchronistic conversations; of teachers and mentors, of social media posts, of new insights that were intuitively guided. I learned so much and in this chapter I share my most significant learnings with you, with the intention of inspiring healing and enhancing your money story, no matter where your starting point.

A frequently recurring question on my reflections is, Why did I need to experience the depths of lack that I did? Because I was experiencing the same depths of misalignment. I'm sure you've seen by now the slow learner and hard lessons theme? It all ties in. Of course now too, with the value of hindsight, I know that every experience is valuable and necessary and that I absolutely needed to experience all of that to become the passionate manifestor that I am today!

#1 and maybe the absolute most important is knowing and truly understanding that we are infinite beings of the universe and we are infinitely abundant. It would a bit woo-woo but trust me! The lack is a fear state we learn in this human experience. Every time we have a money situation be it conversation, exchange or other with someone conditioned to lack, it is stored in our memory bank of money stories. "That's too expensive", "we can't afford that", "Money doesn't grow on trees" etc. it's like our personal library of money stories, except all of the books have the same ending – lack! When we understand frequency, we understand that lack = lower vibrational energy. Where our focus goes, our energy flows. If we keep saying we never have enough money, that will become our reality and on the contrary when we are in the habit of affirming abundance, so it is! Healing our old money stories is an important step in creating a new more abundant relationship with your finances. A powerful journaling ritual around this is to allow yourself to reflect and record all of the experiences of lack that have created the foundation for your existing relationship with money. All of the times you were met with lack and those stories were affirmed. Then go to each on and forgive it. Allow yourself to acknowledge it's role in your story and then let it go. Letting go of these old stories will create space to welcome in more beautiful abundance.

Money is energy, it flows. When we hold too tightly we interrupt it's natural dance, as well as our faith and surrender to the divine process. In our family, we use the analogy of tides to depict our financial flow, we experience high and low tides, we experience king tides, we are in awe and gratitude for the entire process. If we fall into fear (we are human, that does happen!) we come back to the tools in this chapter and devote more time, energy and focus on ensuring our money mindset is good. I have a little anchor in my mind that I love to come back to when I need it. Fear freezes our flow. If I find myself falling into fear, I remember I don't want to freeze the flow that is always incoming to me, so I take some time to consciously re-frame it. Embodied gratitude is a great antidote to fear and a powerful part of our money manifesting. Always be grateful for what you have, for what money you receive, no matter how big or small. If you find five cents on the street, do you stop to pick it up? So many people say no! I say yes, absolutely!!! I am conscious of not allowing my actions to communicate to the universe that I don't want more money. Leaving that 5c creates the story that you don't want or need it.

I found 3x 5c within about five minutes of each other, just the other day. My little loves questioned why I am always so grateful, 'it's only 5c'. I explained that was 15c in just 5 mins. That could be 30c in 10 mins, in an hour I would have almost $2, that's $20 per day! We could keep that going as long as you want to be convinced. But for little to no effort at all, I was gaining abundance. They were mind blown.

The future is yours. Write it well.

The same is true of when we are offered money, whether it be in exchange for a service or a repaying of a debt; I never say no. Sometimes, I will negotiate the amount or strike a different deal but I am conscious to never say 'no thank you'. Money is always welcome to flow to me and I honour it's energy. I remember reading once that 'wasting' $27 per day adds up to $10,000 in a year. Now this isn't some frugal living tips, this is a reminder, to not dismiss even the small amounts of abundance that flow your way, it's all energy and it all adds up.

One of the biggest learnings I had around gratitude with money was paying my bills with gratitude. At the time my main and most painful bill was credit card debt that I had accrued in that misaligned relationship prior to meeting my husband. How was I supposed to find gratitude for that! All I felt was resentment, abandonment and shame. I sat with it because I really wanted to heal those money wounds. And what I came to realise was, every payment was one step closer to finally fully closing off that chapter of my past. After years of dodging phone calls, with this new money healing underway, I answered one of those dreaded phone calls. That call was one of the most life changing of my life! I could not believe my ears. It was the credit card debt collection agency calling to say they had noticed my renewed commitment to meeting my payment arrangement and as a result wanted to offer me a discounted early exit. By aligning with gratitude, I had created space for this new money story to unfold. This was an integral part of my healing journey. Free from the resentment fuelled reminders of that crappy time, I could finally truly begin to heal and to find forgiveness. I couldn't believe it, I had just *began a 21 day money manifesting challenge, the book had suggested $1,000 in 21 days. But in my usual 'go big or go home style', I'd added a 0. and here I was on day 1, already half way to my goal. What else was possible.*

Which brings us seamlessly, again, to surrender. Yes there's that word again! You can't manifest without it! When we are calling in money, we must surrender, we can't control the how. If you try to control where the money will come from, you close yourself off from the potential of income from other places. It's like your narrow vision says a subconscious 'no thank you' to the universe, just the same way as leaving the 5c on the ground does. It is important to remain open and to surrender control of the how. You will always receive exactly what you need to, in divine timing. Now I know first hand how tricky this can be when you're starting out. We are conditioned to a 'believe it when we see it' attitude but in truth the opposite is a manifesting mindset. Believe it and you will see it. We must have faith. And in fairness, if you're broke right now, faith may be all you have. Hold on to that! It will help you through, remember fear will only keep you stuck.

Money is energy, it loves purpose. When giving money a purpose it is important to meet yourself where you are at. Like the two stories I've shared around credit and reclaiming those lack story spaces; it would have been total self sabotage for either my friend or I to begin our money manifesting journey by manifesting a brand new BMW right. What we needed to work on first was clearing the debt that we was already our reality. My credit card freedom was step one of a big journey for my little family. That was our

The future is yours. Write it well.

first stepping stone to realising a dream at the time of buying a house. We knew that to manifest the house we dreamed of, we first needed to tie up some loose ends and heal. Once those initial steps were accomplished, we could then turn our focus more fully to calling the house in. Money loves a purpose, when you are calling money in, get specific about where it will be going and what you will be achieving with it. Focus on the energy that the results will bring and how it will enhance your life or the life of those around you. Can you relate your manifesting desires to the wider collective? the common good of all? The further out of yourself you can ripple the positive impacts of your manifesting results the more power it has. Look at Tony Robbins and his Feed America program. This selfless giving is a wonderful example of how good intention and positive purpose will attract money to the right people. Wealth is way more than your bank balance, wealth is the good that you can do in the world with the abundance that you have called in. What good could you do with the abundance that you are calling in? Remember the importance of embodiment here, how does it feel to be in that abundance? Just like the vision piece in the previous chapter, the more clear and detailed we can be on giving money this purpose the more powerful our manifestation will be.

Another powerful point of clarity is values. If we truly know and understand our values; giving money a purpose will naturally be in alignment with then. The more practised we are the more beneficial and flowing these processes will be for us. The minimalism principles in Chapter 14 tie in here too. For example; someone who places little or no value on their role in environmental issues will value fast fashion clothing choices as much as I value a great op shop find! I recently witnessed a beautiful unfolding of this value aligned spending in my own journey and have used this story to affirm my choices for a little while now. I truly value time, peace and sanity. So when life is busy and time is more precious than abundant; I value the absolute privilege that is eating out. A family member who does not have the same alignment scoffed that we were 'eating out again' and sparked a beautiful reflection of this process for me. We live in a small coastal town, during the off seasons, our local cafes and restaurants rely on locals who value their service and offerings. When we go to the kebab shop we are not only getting a delicious meal, we are supporting our friends small business. Since this reflection hubby and I now say 'let's support (insert biz name)'s business this evening and allow them to cook dinner'. Similarly another friend of mine recently signed up for a new supplement regime which I don't personally see value in for myself, she said the value in it for her is that she is feeling so much more energised, escaping the 3pm slump means that she is more devoted to cooking dinner and therefore saving herself money on allowing our friends in local food business' to cook for her. That decision is so deeply aligned with her current values that the value of where she is sharing her money feels right. Again, it really comes down to embodied gratitude, once you are making aligned decisions and truly feeling deeply grateful for what your money is creating in your life then the flow remains in the higher vibrations and all is well.

The future is yours. Write it well.

> *"It is fun to think on purpose, and even more fun to see the results of those deliberately chosen thoughts"* Esther and Jerry Hicks – Money and the Law of Attraction.

Essentially mindset is key, but so is presence. Do not hide from your money stories. Nor do I encourage in any way a fake it till you make it approach. This kind of tactic all too often goes hand in hand with a 'head in the sand' kind of mindset. I repeat, do not hide from your money stories. Do not avoid the reality of your financial situation, the more upfront, honest and transparent you are with yourself (and in my case my debtors and financial advisers) the better for everyone. Manifesting requires you to get real with yourself. Have faith and face your challenges. Recently I connected with a friend striving to build her business to no avail. Despite her best efforts (yes there were some big pivots around alignment and inspired action!!!) her business simply was not thriving to the level her lifestyle required. I encouraged her to allow her self the time and space to welcome in a super fun and aligned part time job that funded her lifestyle until her business could. She instantly had an incredibly welcomed breathing space and within months of getting her head out of the sand, her business began to grow in beautiful and surprising ways.

There is another important lesson in the example I just shared, while I absolutely encourage you to leave lack behind, I just as strongly encourage you not to live beyond your means while healing these stories. Like in the example above; I read somewhere recently, let your job fund your business until your business can fund your dream. You get the picture.

My Wild and Wonderful Money Stories

On a recent money story healing binge I recorded in real time the stories that presented and the processes they brought so that I could share them here with you and inspire you to look at your own money stories too. Do these sound familiar? Do you allow yourself time and space to truly explore and experience your own money stories? As you will see from the examples below. It is important not only to become aware of the story but also to acknowledge its origin. I love to take time to literally re-write each story as it presents.

"Only main stream jobs yield success, financial reward, public recognition".

This one was laughable to my rational brain. I know so well that not only is this not true but also it is not even remotely aligned with my values. I feel a big part of my mission in this world is to shake things up... this belief was stored deep within my cells from who knows where. While I was on a mission to uncover it's origins, I became more intimate with my own story. Of my belief about jobs and working. I found an opportunity to really align with my own feelings around trading time for money.

The future is yours. Write it well.

Along a similar vein but another belief that needed to be rewritten in it's own right. "I am not worthy of the wealth I am calling in, because I haven't worked hard enough". I know I have touched on this time and time again, the worthiness piece, the judgement of others, the unseen 'work' of this manifesting life and here it is again, in another context! I absolutely don't even rationally believe this. I know that manifesting magic transcends time and space, that it is ultimately a universal abundance frequency that I am tapping in to. I am sharing these experiences to let you know that you are not alone in the challenges you face and to show you practical ways of working through the blocks.

It is important to note my process here, when I identify these limiting beliefs, I create time and space to find their source. Simply asking where did this belief come from? and seeing the story that they have created in my life. How have these beliefs impacted my action or indeed inaction. I also explore the 'truth' of them and the gratitude for them. For example, my old story of me being bad with money, that I can't be trusted with money because I make financial 'mistakes' was rooted in judgements and opinions of others. Because previously my actions with money were not aligned with their truth, circumstances or values. My old limiting belief that 'people with lots of money are full of themselves' serves me in one way because those judgements keep me humble and relatable no matter how abundant that high tide is.

Another huge can of worms that I opened for myself in my recent money story healing was around privacy... money needs to be private, if I share I will be exposed. I realised that I am always holding on to some fear-based emotion around money. If I am in a low tide; shame. If I am in high tide; guilt. In those old stories I couldn't win! My mantra now is "I am free from financial shame and guilt". These stories created such stagnance and ebb and flow for me. I realised that I have been hiding behind this 'private' money story for so long; if I am rich I will have no excuses! Those excuses range from pretty reasonable to downright outrageous! This money privacy part also extended to feeling more relatable to others. People generally speak more openly about money struggles than they do about high tides; it is what we are conditioned to do. You can't be seen to be too full of yourself or to celebrate too much, I'm sure you're seeing it but these beliefs are all so complexly interconnected, interwoven and intertwined so that determining the source and story can require some brave self reflection work! Its not always an easy or quick fix process, but as will all of these processes, it is absolutely worth it! I now affirm that I am an alchemist, part of my role here is to change these stories, to have these conversations to encourage us to bravely see the truth of and rewrite our money stories.

This work is ongoing. Consistency is key. We must continue to revisit these themes over and over again. As will all area's and elements of this healing journey. Every time we return to a familiar process we are doing so from a new perspective, with more knowing than we had last time.

The future is yours. Write it well.

My Go-To Regular Money Manifesting Rituals

Now I want to share with you some of my favourite regular money manifesting rituals. When I am cleaning and cleansing my home, I include my wallet. I tidy it out, clean it and smoke cleanse it regularly, I always strive to ensure that I have cash in there at all times. Preferably a $50 or $100 note to remind me of abundance and my abundant mindset every time I open it. I affirm, listen to and sing money mantras to myself daily; if I am on a particularly focused money manifesting journey I set reminders on my phone to pop up and refocus my mindset at various times through out the day. With money based affirmations, I particularly love melodic mantras like "Money is Coming to me" by Karen Drucker, I love that vibe. I also highly recommend a wonderful book called "Manifest Your Inner Money Babe" by Katherine Zinker. That is my go to when I am manifesting big goals. There are so many amazing resources, give yourself permission to be open to transcend your money stories and welcome in the correctly aligned information that will come to you in divine timing.

Above all, what I want you to take away from this chapter of the book is an unwavering belief that YOU ARE WORTHY!!! If that triggers any doubt or discomfort in you, I encourage you to explore why? Where is the old story of unworthiness originating from or rooted in? Now, is your time to see the truth of that situation and to heal that wound. Sometimes all we need is permission to do things differently.... Here is your permission!

Chapter 19

Raising Sensitive Souls

To be honest I questioned if this chapter was going to be another book in its own right, it is something that I am so passionate about and have so much to share. I see now that it is the perfect closing to this 'chapter' of our journey together. This is where I am at, right now, at present. It is a story of my current triggers, healings and indeed, of my becoming. Every moment of my life has led me to this and this is one area that I show up fully, every day, with all of my heart.

> "Have a heart that never hardens, and a temper that never tires, and a touch that never hurts" Charles Dickens.

One thing I knew without a doubt for as long as I can remember was that I wanted, beyond anything, to be a mammy. It was like my heart was exploding with love to give and I was just waiting for my little people to come along for me to give it.... hard, every day! Raising my children has been one of the most challenging, rewarding, confronting, deeply healing adventures I've ever signed up for and I embrace every messy moment of it. They are my greatest teachers, my most astute accountability partners and my greatest loves. As I tucked these little loves into bed one night while writing this book, I was overwhelmed with emotion. "You are just so beautiful" I thought, "I wish you could see yourself through my eyes"! It instantly cast my mind back to the time when I yearned for this love. For as long as I can remember, I called you in, I dreamed of you, I wished for you. You are one of my most powerful manifestations of my life.

Bringing these beautiful little star seeds into the world was one of the most life-changing experiences I could have ever asked for, my first born were my twins. Their birth, far from the fairy tale I had wished for, the universe had other plans and our epic healing journey began then. While loving and forgiving my dis-empowered and unknowing self, I often find myself unconsciously thinking that I wish I knew then what I know now. A beautiful nod to the wonderfully empowered mamas in my circle now, who free birth, and how awe-inspiring their stories are! But the simple truth is, I didn't. And that in itself is perfect. I feel that our traumatic experience was my first rite as a mother who would fiercely lead her daughters to believe in themselves above all else, to trust their intuition, and to honour the truth of their soul. Much of my healing in the past nine years has been driven by and devoted to this journey of motherhood.

Becoming a mother really amplified my appreciation for the women who raised me. Raising a child is a labour of love, raising a sensitive child is confronting, raising a child that's not yours is commendable, raising a highly sensitive child that not yours is a whole other level of love and commitment. Seriously, I know, through years of introspection and self-reflection that I was not an easy child to raise. I feel that many of those challenges are coming back to me from my children now so that I can see and heal those elements of childhood me that still need nurturing and tending to. My children are incredibly clingy, as was I, largely due to the abandonment wounds that I experienced in childhood. They don't sleep through the night, or in their own beds, as I didn't. They have separation anxiety and fear every time I leave, even for an hour, that something bad will happen and I will never return. I literally relive those feelings in my own body every time I see it triggered in theirs. It is wild how our own traumas can imprint on our little people. While I nurture them through their triggers and empower them to be less fearful of the 'what if's', I simultaneously work on healing my own wounds. Keeping in mind their sensitivity and incredible connection to my energy. When we do the healing work it is believed that we are healing seven generations around us; forward and back! I truly see this play out, in real time, often. I can be deep in a healing process on the other side of the world and I will get a call or text from my family in Ireland sharing thoughts or feelings that have 'randomly' popped up for them. The power of this healing is WILD and should never be overlooked.

Self-Criticism and Self-Judgement

One of the greatest points of healing on this journey as a mother, has been becoming aware of just how critical and fearful I am of judgement. My fear of judgement from others has made me incredibly self-critical. *That old familiar "They'll say" story that plays over and over in my head, has contributed to being quite an anxious parent. Just the other day a friend was telling me that she had a scary moment when her child was young and she realised 'in hindsight' that she probably shouldn't have been quite as brave adventure mama as she was that day. I marvelled, as I do at these brave mama's who do courageous things with their young children. I hadn't fully seen, until that moment how much this criticism wounding was holding me back. I am much more a no thank you, I'd rather sit on the side line, wishing I was that brave but debating with that voice in my head that always tells me "what will they say if it all goes wrong". I am passionate about raising courageous young people who fully trust themselves and their ability to adventure. Quite the opposite to their mama, and I realise now that I have not been modelling or energetically supporting that very well. Now the silver lining of all of this is of course, awareness. But also, knowing deep down that all of my big decisions and choices are well thought out. I am often judged as reckless or living with 'too much' abandon, but that actually couldn't be further from the truth. I have developed such a strong and unwavering bond with my intuition that when faced with big decisions, I trust it fully to guide me in the right direction. I know deeply, that even in the face of a challenge, I am always held. I can navigate tricky life situations and I can do so with grace and peace. I know deeply that I came here, to this place where I currently call home, to be held so deeply in the sisterhood here while I heal and unravel these pieces of me. I can hear voices of dear friends reminding me so often to be gentle with myself to give myself a break to see the beautiful job that I am doing of life. And their voices are empowering my self compassionate voice, encouraging her out of the dark, allowing her to be louder that the self critical voice that began to dominate again at some stage, unknown. It is beautiful in its unfolding and as with all healing, I can more clearly see the role that I played in this whole looping criticism story.*

> **'I do not allow anyone else to dim my light. Why am I suddenly accepting that from myself'. From the path of light journal.**

The little voice in my head looped the 'you're so self-righteous' affirmation that had been directed toward me during a significant traumatic event in my life. Over the years, I became so fearful of that judgement. Shrinking into people pleasing and choosing to blend in rather than being seen. When my children were born, I knew that something needed to change if I were to model the empowerment that I wished for them. I began, a conscious journey of thinking for myself. As Socrates said 'To find yourself, *think for yourself*. I realised that I had been living in other peoples paradigms and despite the extended 'teenage' rebellion, I was a lost soul, searching for her home. What I didn't know then, was that this home that I yearned for was within me. My children cracked my heart open and illuminated the way.

Now this is not to say that the judgement of others doesn't still play on my mind sometimes, but as with the example above of my wonderful village of wise women; I interrupt that loop with the reassurance and realignment with the truth that I am on the right path. To stay on this path I have learned that I must not give my power away to others. I must not allow their judgement or opinions to sway me. When I am deeply aligned with my values and devoted to my daily rhythms that support that, I am much harder to sway off course! This is the grounded spirituality that I intend to leave as my legacy for my children. 'Live firmly in your own truth and do no harm to others'.

I remember the first day the universe really nudged me to do this in a big way. I had dropped the girls off at kindy and called a dear friend crying my eyes out. My littlest twins separation anxiety was at an all time peak and I could not bear leaving her there crying. I was exhausted and grateful for the break but I couldn't help but feel like I was doing my daughter an injustice forcing her to be separated from me. All of the contemporary parenting stuff said it was the right thing to do, they will build resilience, blah blah blah. But it just felt so wrong for me! My friend tenderly talked me through what she could see from an outsiders perspective and I went home to have a big conversation with hubby.

The future is yours. Write it well.

That was her last day of kindy! Her sister stayed on for the remaining few months and both girls started prep together the following year. I wasn't sure on school, my desire for home school life growing by the day. Finally, after some pretty big struggles during their prep year, I plucked up the courage to just give it a go. One of their teachers reassuring me that if it didn't work out, they could always come back! I hadn't thought of it like that. Everything in my life to that point had always been so all or nothing. This flow and pivot was kind of new territory for me. Quickly, it became a familiar dance and now is the energetic by which I live my life. We flow with the energies of our family and pivot as we need to, to honour where we are at and what we need in the moment. There is no more 'shoulds' or 'have to's' and seriously everyone is thriving.

Homeschooling life is not for everyone, and I would be lying if I said every day was a walk in the park. Some days are incredibly tough, but those days are easily outweighed by the good ones. This year I learned first hand the importance of looking after myself and my own mental health as a priority. It had been a tough year all round, with so many deaths of loved ones in one year and I lost myself in the process of grief. I had given myself grace to just go through the motions, but I'd kind of forgotten to get back on the track after a period of time. I was fading fast and my relationship with my family reflected that. We were not making time for the things we love enough, there was constant bickering and fighting among the kids and a general sense of disconnect that felt like it was spiralling. I am so glad that I caught it, before it went too far, and that I have the tools to lean on to get myself back into alignment and flowing again with the higher vibrational energies.

During those darker days my shadow introspection was at another level and so much of my own unhealed wounds had been revealed and resurfaced for me. Where the kids were triggering me, I didn't find my usual opportunities for learning, I found deep wounds that were marinading in a stew of self-criticism and fear. Oh the fear! The fears were irrational and I was manifesting against myself! I was forced to revisit all of the times that I'd dis-empowered myself, that I'd made misaligned choices, that I chose to run and hide instead of stand in my power and speaking up and being heard. Why? Why did I need to go through all of this again and again? What lessons had I missed. And then it hit me, a yearning to return home, to my motherland to truly integrate the healing that I had been so devoted to since my departure 17 years ago. The ghosts of my past were calling me to confront them, bravely and empowered. It was time to sew the final threads of that healing chapter into my tapestry of life. To return to the place where I first learned of love, to feel that again. To feel the warmth of my family and the heart beat of that sacred land. It was like the souls of my children were yearning for it and so, preparation for the next chapter of our story began.

'Where ever you go, go with all your heart'
Confucius

A Parting Note

'A good book has no ending' Robert Dalziel Cumming.

We don't need to have it all figured out. There is a poetic beauty to surrendering to the unknown.

Why do we feel like we need to have it all mapped out. If we are too rigid in our plans, there is no room for adventure. My gypsy soul wants the enchantment of the path less known. 'There is a pleasure in the pathless woods' Lord Byron. Don't get too caught up on always knowing the next step. If you feel called or guided, take a leap.

'Our true destination's not marked on any charts, we're navigating to the shores of the heart' Christy Moore 'The Voyage'.

Life is an adventure. It is here to be lived. We never know which day will be our last. It's short and nothing is guaranteed, don't worry about what people will think or how something will look. If you are truly aligned with your values, if your intentions are for the greatest good, trust yourself beyond all else.

The Voyage – Christy Moore
I am a sailor, you're my first mate
We signed on together, we coupled our fate
Hauled up our anchor, determined not to fail
For the hearts treasure, together we set sail
With no maps to guide us we steered our own course
Rode out the storms when the winds were gale force
Sat out the doldrums in patience and hope
Working together we learned how to cope

Life is an ocean and love is a boat
In troubled water that keeps us afloat
When we started the voyage, there was just me and you
Now gathered round us, we have our own crew

Together we're in this relationship
We built it with care to last the whole trip
Our true destination's not marked on any charts
We're navigating to the shores of the heart

Life is an ocean and love is a boat
In troubled water that keeps us afloat
When we started the voyage, there was just me and you
Now gathered round us, we have our own crew

Life is an ocean and love is a boat
In troubled water that keeps us afloat
When we started the voyage, there was just me and you
Now gathered round us, we have our own crew

My heart absolutely overflows with gratitude...

To my wonderful and patient husband and his endless support of these wild ideas (and the sleepless nights that usually come with them!). I am forever grateful that we chose this voyage together and that we do it with such grace. You are my number one cheerleader and cup of tea maker. You are always by my side.

To my beautiful little family for enduring the endless hours of me 'in the zone' with my journal or laptop frantically scrawling as this flowed through me. For running with another crazy Claire idea and for feeding me, supporting me and giving me the space I needed to bring this to life.

To my beautiful children for inspiring me to be brave, to be passionate and to chase my dreams with abandon. I said above that dad is my number one cheerleader but in all honesty, I have a whole cheer squad. You guys are my biggest inspiration and my greatest critics. You keep me grounded, centred and flowing. I love you.

To my Irish family, without you I wouldn't be a shadow of the person I am today. Your endless years of sleepless nights and challenging behaviour endurance shaped the bravery I embody today.

To my Innamincka fam, for opening your hearts and home to us. For the space holding, cacao making, child minding, hand holding, the proof reading, the honesty and the absolute unconditional love. 'I can't believe we've manifested this!!!' (our favourite catch phrase, almost daily).

To my childhood sweetheart who is no longer with us, for always encouraging me not to give a fuck what others think and do the things anyway! Our friendship endured the years and got stronger as we forged our lives independently. Your parting gift, were the most powerful and healing words, that I never knew I needed. Your legacy you left behind continues to encourage and guide me everyday.

To Adrianne, my boss lady, my mentor and my biggest fan. Your endless encouragement and direct 'heart on your sleeve' communication is what has brought this book to life. We are both teacher and student always. Our friendship reminds me of this in every chapter.

To my team of 'book birth doulas', you held me so encouragingly through out this process. Your messages always so timely and your feedback always progressive. To Tara & "the Rachels" for your incredible attention to detail in all of the waves of editing. For the tender care with which you held my words, the butt-kicking chats, the heart-centred guidance and the laughs along the way.

To my Claire Roe Wellness community for being the audience that brought this story to life. For having faith in my work and my teaching, for seeing me and holding me through all of the pivots, all of these years, with so much love.

To my local Aggie girl gang, my field of wildflowers, what an epic cheer squad. There simply are no words for how amazing each and every one of you are.

To you, reading this. Thank you from the depths of my infinite divinely connected heart. I hope that after this journey together you see me. You see me in you, you in me and that you feel inspired and empowered to manifest your wildest dreams.

With so much love and heart-FULL gratitude,

Claire Roe

(now officially an author!!!)